SHRINKING ELEPHANTS

*To my growing band of elephant shrinkers.
Never give up hope that we can transform this
world, one conversation at a time.*

ABOUT THE AUTHOR

Genevieve Hawkins has a unique combination of skills in health, human behaviour and commercial business at small and large scale. She published her first book, Mentally at Work, while working full time in an executive role, as she saw a need in the marketplace to give leaders a pragmatic way of looking after their own mental health and influencing that of the organisation they work in. It took off far more than she had expected and has been humbled by the feedback she has been given on its impact on people's lives. While she had never thought she would write a second book, both the response from her first, and the continuing elephants in the room in workplaces, got her energised to want to write this second book. Again, focused on pragmatic ways of helping leaders develop the critical skill of having better conversations to find common understanding and unlock value. When she isn't writing, or working with businesses to improve commercial collaboration, Genevieve helps leaders have the conversations they need to have, including with themselves.

SHRINKING ELEPHANTS

———

Untangling workplace conflict
to unlock value for all

GENEVIEVE HAWKINS

First published in 2024 by Mentally at Work, Melbourne, Australia.

© Genevieve Hawkins 2024

The moral rights of the author have been asserted.

All rights reserved. Except as permitted under the Australian Copyright Act 1968 (For example: a fair dealing for the purposes of study, research, criticism or review.) No part of this book may be reproduced, stored within a retrieval system, communicated or transmitted in any form without prior written permission. All inquiries should be made to the publisher at enquiries@mentallyatwork.com.au

Book design: Ckaos
Printer: Ingram Spark, Australia

ISBN: 978-1-7636703-0-3

Disclaimer: The material throughout this publication is only representative of general comments, instead of professional advice. Its intention is not to provide specific guidance for any particular circumstances. It should not be relied upon for any decision to take action or not to take action on any matter which it covers. Readers should obtain professional advice wherever appropriate, and before making any such decision. To the maximum extent permitted by law, the author and publisher disclaim all responsibility and liability to any person, arising directly or indirectly from any person taking or not taking action based on the information in this book.

CONTENTS

	Foreword	ix
INTRODUCTION	Is there an elephant in the room?	1
SECTION ONE	Where does conflict come from?	9
CHAPTER ONE	There isn't an elephant	10
CHAPTER TWO	How your brain grows elephants	31
CHAPTER THREE	Spotting common elephants	50
SECTION TWO	Can you stop it before it grows?	79
CHAPTER FOUR	The support you need to shrink elephants	80
CHAPTER FIVE	The Five Principles of shrinking an elephant	95
CHAPTER SIX	Let's shrink an elephant	115
SECTION THREE	Can you stay curious when it is big?	149
CHAPTER SEVEN	Walking with big elephants	150
CHAPTER EIGHT	When you contribute to growing a big elephant	168
CHAPTER NINE	Scaling elephant shrinking	188
NEXT STEPS	Your commitment to shrinking elephants to unlock value	206
	Your ready reckoner	213
	Acknowledgements	217

FOREWORD

When Russian poet Ivan Krylov wrote "The Inquisitive Man" in the 18th century, he tells the story of a man who goes to a museum and notices all sorts of little things but fails to notice an elephant. While he couldn't have predicted that his elephant would become the proverbial "elephant in the room" centuries later, the poem gave us a clue as to the potential dangers that occur in relationships when we're not inquisitive, and in a rush to be right, fail to tap into arguably the most powerful tool for human connection... curiosity!

Later that same century another poet, Walt Whitman, coined a phrase that Ted Lasso recently made famous; "be curious not judgemental". But neither Ivan, Walt (nor Ted) gave us the tools on how to actually do that, especially at work.

Enter Genevieve Hawkins and Shrinking Elephants. An important and necessary book, that encapsulates how to use curiosity, vulnerability and a bit of science, to shrink the elephant in the room. Creating the critical skills for genuine human connection and understanding, especially at work. Through structured questions and simple frameworks, Genevieve explains how to have open conversations that enables us to play with elephants in a room, rather than fear them.

Curiosity is a "play" state, and humans are designed by nature to play. The opposite of play is not work – the opposite of play is fear. Unfortunately, today with our reptilian brains with a negative bias, there is so much fear inside organisations, that we are losing our competitive advantage as a species. Which is why Shrinking Elephants is such an important book for our times.

In the same way that Genevieve's best-selling first book (which I binged in a day), 'Mentally at Work', gave us the mental health skills to connect with ourselves first, before we connect with others, Shrinking Elephants gives us the critical skills to create an open and open-minded working environment. Where talking about our different perspectives honestly, shrinks elephants, enhancing trust, empowerment and alignment.

At its core, Genevieve reminds us that "perspective" is the way we see something. As meaning-makers, we are the stories we tell ourselves about ourselves. But our stories are not necessarily accurate, right or true. With the right skills and toolkit, we can be "caring scientists" to gently explore firstly our own stories and then those of our colleagues.

In organisational culture, disagreement can be a good thing. As it often creates a healthy tension, where innovation blossoms, through the intersection of different views coming together. But without a common language and the right skills, disagreement so often turns to conflict, and as we are typically conflict-avoiders, elephants can grow big and silent and dangerous. But as Genevieve points out, with simple techniques we can walk with elephants and learn their ways. And even learn to shrink them.

We can also observe if we are the ones creating elephants. Note to author… I have already put a sticky note on my computer that says, "Accept multiple truths" to ask myself 'how might I be wrong?' Seeking evidence that supports how I may be wrong, so I can accept multiple truths about an elephant, is a work in progress though.

One of the most powerful aspects of Shrinking Elephants is teaching us how to walk with elephants with compassion, empathy and generous assumptions, rather than silence, violence and cortisol-fuelled judgements. It helps us discover we have so much more power than we realise, to take control of tricky situations when they arise. That it's not what happens to us in life that matters, but rather how we respond to what happens to us in life, that truly matters. It's always about the response.

One of my favourite mantras that has guided me my whole life is "you can't control the waves, but you can learn to surf". Shrinking Elephants reminds us that as long as we remain open, vulnerable and playful, we can walk with elephants and learn their ways. Turning conflict, into meaningful disagreements. Because learning, growth and potential so often comes from meaningful disagreements, where different points of view can co-exist to create a better future.

Bravo Genevieve, and those brave enough to follow her lead.

Ben Crowe
Professional Mentor
Founder of Mojo Crowe

INTRODUCTION – IS THERE AN ELEPHANT IN THE ROOM?

Conflict is an opportunity. Use it wisely and you will unlock value in you, your team and your organisation.

Conflict exists in every organisation. Sometimes very obviously. Sometimes quietly. Very few love it. Thank you, therefore, for being curious enough to pick up Shrinking Elephants and wonder what might be inside the cover.

How many of these thoughts (or similar thoughts) have you had in your working life, but not taken practical action to resolve?
- It is unreasonable to think we can deliver high quality outcomes with the cost pressures we are under. Everyone is feeling it. No one is saying it.
- Whenever I see them walking into the room, I can feel my guard go up and tension build.

- These systems are so frustrating but there is nothing you can do about them.
- We agreed on what we would do in the meeting, but people are doing something different.
- They are not capable of delivering what is needed but no one is doing anything about it.
- I am not getting the support I need, but it is too risky to ask for help. I'll be criticised and that's career limiting.

This is quiet conflict. It exists in every organisation. It is typically ignored. Or whispered about, behind closed doors. It causes tension in individuals and energy to leak from the organisation. Slowing down the organisation and its desired performance.

> 'Fear grips most corporate cultures: fear of losing control of the outcome, looking stupid, or being judged... Withholding creates serious problems for teams. Relevant information isn't shared. The best decisions aren't made. Once decisions are made, people aren't fully aligned, leading to the "meeting after the meeting". Most importantly, when people withhold, it drains their energy and creativity.'[*]

Accepting quiet conflict, is choosing to live with fear. It is accepting an organisation with blockages. An organisation that doesn't reach its potential. People that don't reach their potential.

We all come to the table with our different perspectives, from our own unique life experiences. When you don't truly understand and accept these differences, it can be like standing at opposite ends of a very large elephant. Different perspectives, when respectfully listened to and considered, can help solve complex problems. Different perspectives, when not spoken, ignored,

---

[*] Zhang, E. (June 5, 2024). Verge Genomics CEO: Why I urge my employees to share their fears and vulnerabilities – and do the same with them. Fortune.com

INTRODUCTION

dismissed, or at worse, ridiculed, lead to growing elephants that cause conflict.

Unresolved conflict erodes confidence, health and performance by stealth.

To make things more complicated, we now live in a VUCA (volatile, uncertain, complex, ambiguous) world. Volatility and uncertainty place strain on our collective mental health. The complexity and ambiguity we face, need a level of collaboration we have never been able to achieve before.

'Just as people one hundred years ago underwent a profound change in how they thought about the way work gets done, today's turbulent work environment once again requires a new mindset – not just new slogans. It requires a new way of thinking.'*

We do not exist in the world of the sole 'hero' anymore. No one person, or department, or organisation, will have the answers to the complex problems we have. Collaboration is the only way. Across and between organisations. Collaboration comes from deep trust. Deep trust comes from choosing not to fear the elephants. Rather learning how to collectively shrink them so you can harness differences to better solve problems. You cannot continue to accept the elephant in the room and push on, if you want to lead sustainably in a VUCA world. You need to develop the skills to navigate, what can be clunky conversations, to shrink elephants. Untangling the quiet conflict, before it grows to loud, difficult conflict.

Welcome to Shrinking Elephants. A book linking science and pragmatism, to the real world of business. It will help you untan-

---

* Edmonson, A. (2012). Teaming: How Organizations Learn, Innovate, and Compete in the Knowledge Economy. John Wiley & Sons Inc. San Francisco, CA, USA.

gle both quiet and loud conflict in the workplace. This is not a standard conflict resolution book. Rather this is a book that focuses on understanding how elephants form and grow. It will help you build skills in shrinking them before they lead to loud conflict. Although, yes, I will help you understand what to do if the conflict does get louder.

Don't fear the elephant. In it lies your potential and the potential of the organisation.

Why listen to me?

I have been shrinking elephants over a 30-year career. I started my career as a clinical Occupational Therapist. This, along with a personal relationship struggle at that time, is where the microchip got inserted in me. I was curious that we can have such different perspectives on the one situation and not be able to reconcile them.

Spending a significant proportion of my career in personal injury management, I have seen the impacts of elephants that were ignored. Of people who hadn't felt heard and lashed out. Of relationships that unnecessarily broke down. Of careers cut short. Of health that didn't fully recover. I would often be involved at the tail end, where there were limited actions that could be taken to repair relationships. It frustrated me. I have also helped people resolve these differences, to lead healthier, happier lives and work more effectively together. I consistently saw the value of shrinking elephants.

Fast forwards post my OT and consulting days, and further post graduate studies, in occupational hazards, change and business management, I became a commercial executive. I was leading major commercial transformations in large, complex organisations. Change inevitably causes discomfort. I continued to hone my elephant shrinking skills, using my combination of health, behaviour and commercial skills. Through this, I came to appreciate more fully, the dynamics within organisations that grow elephants. The culture of organisations further complicates the stories we all bring to any relationship. I witnessed how not being able to articulate our hidden stories when faced with complex change, grows very big elephants. Elephants that interfered with commercial outcomes. They distracted people. They had people not caring or putting in that extra effort. They impacted careers and health. There were elephants that resulted in people choosing to leave organisations, not enabling them to reach their potential.

This book contains thirty years of experience, that I wish I had in my tool kit a long time ago. I have seen the value that has been unlocked in me, my teams and the organisations I have worked in, when people understand and shrink elephants together. This skill is critical, in our VUCA world. I want to share my experiences with you, to help you learn this skill, to grow as an impactful leader faster.

Why you?

You may have picked up this book because you were just curious about the title. You may not believe you have experienced elephants. You may already sense the elephants. Feeling frustrated with others and the stalemate it causes.

If you are frustrated with yourself for not stepping in; with others, for not playing ball; with the politics that get in the way of getting results; with the clearly dysfunctional teams; then this book is for you. While it is written specifically for those leading teams, anyone can apply the tools within it. I want to help you get more comfortable with identifying elephants in the quiet conflict. Shrinking them, before they cause real problems. While also being confident to face the big ones you may stumble into. When you can understand how your brain naturally works and overlay that with a willingness to learn about yourself, the ecosystem in which you work, and the stories that others have, you will start to realise your full potential as a leader.

What's coming up?

I have divided this book into three sections, each of three chapters:
- **Section One: 'Where does conflict come from?'**, looks at where elephants naturally and unnaturally grow (believe it or not, you can be unconsciously contributing to growing them, as much as anyone). This section helps you identify elephants and the impact on mental health and performance when they aren't managed. It includes some simple strategies to start navigating around elephants together, to prevent conflict in the first place.
- **Section Two: 'Can you stop it before it grows?'**, gives you practical strategies to address quiet conflict early, through helping people learn the shape of these elephants; owning their own role in shrinking them, before they get too unwieldy or entrenched.

INTRODUCTION

- **Section Three: 'Can you stay curious when it's big?'** extends your learning further by stepping into the uncomfortable space of louder conflict with potential legal/career implications, for others and then for you. In the final chapter, I will give you practical tools to take a lead in developing your team to all become conflict-confident elephant shrinkers. This is where it gets big. Decreasing social conflict, while increasing creative conflict. Through this, you will truly unlock the value of the individuals you are working with, so together you can have a much bigger impact than you have ever dreamed of.

In applying the practical tools in this book, you will:
- Learn how to identify the elephants that are blocking effective problem solving and delivery in the workplace.
- Start to understand the underlying unconscious reactions and blind spots, that are at the heart of growing elephants.
- Build confidence in elephant shrinking, that helps you learn about yourself, build trust-based relationships, and stop wasted energy in your organisation.
- Know how to look after yourself and others, through louder conflict issues, coming out the better for it.
- Scale elephant shrinking in your team.

I would encourage you to take the time, to read the book from cover to cover first. Get the foundation you need, to use the science to your advantage. Then use 'Key things to remember' in each chapter, and the Ready Reckoner at the back, as a quick reference guide, when you are choosing to navigate an elephant. If you don't use one already, buy a journal. Use this throughout reading this book. Write down your own reflections and insights. This, along with perhaps a range of sticky notes on this book, will help you learn to be a conflict-confident, elephant shrinking leader, faster.

This book is not about how to do a psychological risk assessment in the workplace. Nor does it guide you, on what does and does not constitute bullying and harassment. You will need to seek out your safety and human resources teams to help you with this legal information. Rather, this book is your guide to recognising conflict within yourself, and with others, when it is quiet. It gives a practical, human-centric approach to get you to a full, triangulated, 3D version of the elephant, faster. A shared, understanding and acceptance of all the different angles that shrinks the elephant to a valuable size.

There will always be elephants. But there is so much to be learnt and unlocked by understanding and ultimately shrinking them. Both for you, as an individual, and the organisation you are working in. I know I am better as a leader and a human being, for seeking to understand the elephants that I have come across. I continue to learn about myself. How I show up. My blind spots that have contributed to elephant growth. I have also unlocked others potential, through my willingness to step in, name the elephant and get people curious.

'Courage is not the absence of fear. Courage is fear walking.'[*]

Elephants are not so scary when you learn their ways. Don't fear them. Take a deep breath and start walking with them. You will be amazed at the value you unlock.

---

[*] David, S PhD. (2016) Emotional Agility: Get Unstuck, Embrace Change, and Thrive in Work and Life. Avery, Penguin Random House LLC. New York. USA.

SECTION ONE

WHERE DOES CONFLICT COME FROM?

CHAPTER ONE

THERE ISN'T AN ELEPHANT!

'Our problem is we are just trying to do too much. We just need to prioritise!'

It felt like Groundhog Day. It was different people, different room, different manager, same elephant. We were up against it in delivering to the budget. There was absolute agreement. There was too much on the plate. We needed to prioritise. There was much hope at the time of the meeting, that this was finally it. It was crunch-time. We would make some tough decisions. On the surface it looked like we had. We had removed some projects, but not enough (and had one added in for good measure). Everyone was focused on what they believed was most important to achieve the vision. But we didn't cut deep enough. There was no obvious dysfunctional conflict in the room. There was good intent. Why couldn't we prioritise? We had a manager saying we needed to prioritise. Yet, each project in isolation was a good one that couldn't be let go. No one, including the manager, was prepared to make the tough calls. Everyone walked out of the long meeting and nothing had really changed. We still had an agenda beyond our capacity. There were whispers of frustration post meeting. It was just another day in the office. There was an elephant in the room no one wanted to talk about.

People can live their lives in denial of the elephants in the room. 'That is just the way it is'. They are only prepared to whisper to others about their frustrations, behind closed doors. Let's face it, it is much simpler to blame the individual, THAT team, or the system or process as 'the problem'. Rather than the conversation that isn't being had. People ignore the internal tension that is building up. The values clashes. They just battle on. Not understanding or believing they can change it. Not appreciating the complexity of the elephant, growing quietly in the room. Blocking the potential of the team and the organisation.

So, let's start exploring those three 'problems' in Chapter One:
- The 'problem' person.
- The team dynamic.
- The organisation you are operating within.

This will help you identify where elephants could exist.

Then, for good measure, the final section of Chapter One will touch on your potential contribution to them.

The problem is THAT person

You have been here before. You can identify people who are 'problems' from a mile away. 'Problem people' drain your energy. Common complaints can be:
- They don't hold themselves accountable
- They aren't in the right role
- It is their personality
- They don't have any insight

Is this an elephant? Maybe. Maybe not. It depends on whether you address the issue or not.

Why don't people do what you want/expect them to do? If you start with a reasonable assumption that people don't go to work to deliberately do the wrong thing, then there must be something much deeper at play. If you can create the environment in which your team hold themselves to account, you avoid creating many elephants in the first place.

I find it useful to consider the Five Cs that need to be present for people to hold themselves to account for what is expected of them (see Figure 1). If they aren't holding themselves to account, you can change that. You can stop an elephant from growing.

FIGURE ONE

The 5 Cs of Accountability
– are they all present?

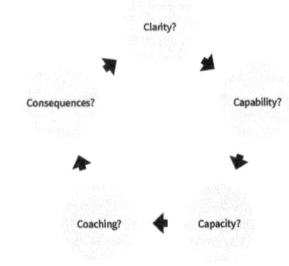

PRACTICAL STEPS:

How you help people to hold themselves accountable

When someone isn't holding themselves to account to deliver as expected, ask yourself the following questions?

1. **Clarity**: Have I been clear on what I need them to do and how it relates to/impacts on what others are doing?
2. **Capability**: Have I recruited for the right skills for this job?
3. **Capacity**: Have I provided them with enough time/resources?
4. **Coaching**: Have I made the environment safe to fail and learn in, so they have the courage to go further? Am I encouraging them through curious questions when they don't quite know what to do to help them learn?
5. **Consequences**: Am I measuring them objectively on what they do, recognising them for delivering or being clear on where I need change? Am I supporting them, so they understand the guardrails they are operating between? Do they feel encouraged and energised?

When you are frustrated with someone else for not doing what you want them to do, the ball is in your court to help shift them into the right mindset as their leader. When they aren't in your team, you can still influence them with this framework, with the one exception of not having the right skills. This is where you then provide this framework to their manager. Help them make the decisions they need to make.

Accountability and fitting people into the right role are the easy part. This is a legitimate problem in workplaces. The Five Cs will help you address it. If you do, there isn't an elephant. What is harder to address is when you think that 'it's their personality'. The American Psychological Society defines personality as 'the enduring characteristics and behaviours that comprise a person's unique adjustment to life, including major traits, interests, drives, values, self-concept, abilities, and emotional patterns'*. Wow, there is a lot to unpack there! On that definition, every single one of us has a unique combination of these things. No wonder this could be the problem! However, blaming someone's personality as *the* issue, not exploring differences, creates an elephant.

Diversity of experience and ways of processing can help produce much better results, but they can cause tension. When someone approaches a situation in a different way to you, yes you could say 'it is a personality clash'. That doesn't mean though, that they are inherently flawed in the way they are doing things. Not exploring this further, creates an elephant.

In considering your frustrations with an individual's personality, reflect on this thing called life. Life is messy for all of us. It rarely goes to plan. Sometimes, the way in which people are responding, is because of what else is happening in their life. The cumulative burden of chronic stress (our allostatic load)†. It could be as simple as not getting a good night's sleep. As complex as a relationship breakdown or serious health issues, combined with increased pressure at work. The saying 'it was the last straw that broke the camel's back' is a useful way of thinking of allostatic load. Sometimes, people just won't show up as their best.

While it would be so much easier if people could just 'get on with their jobs', everyone brings themselves to work. Even when they try to hide it. Reflect on yourself. If you have a very sick child/partner/parent, or you have just lost out on a big investment, or you aren't hitting the targets you expected to hit, how 'in the game' do you honestly think you are? Everyone is different. Everyone brings baggage. Not everyone is suited to the job they are in. All

---

* apa.org/Home/Psychology topics/Personality
† Guidi J, Lucente M, Sonino N, Fava GA. Allostatic Load and Its Impact on Health: A Systematic Review. Psychother Psychosom. 2021;90(1):11–27. doi: 10.1159/000510696. Epub 2020 Aug 14. PMID: 32799204.

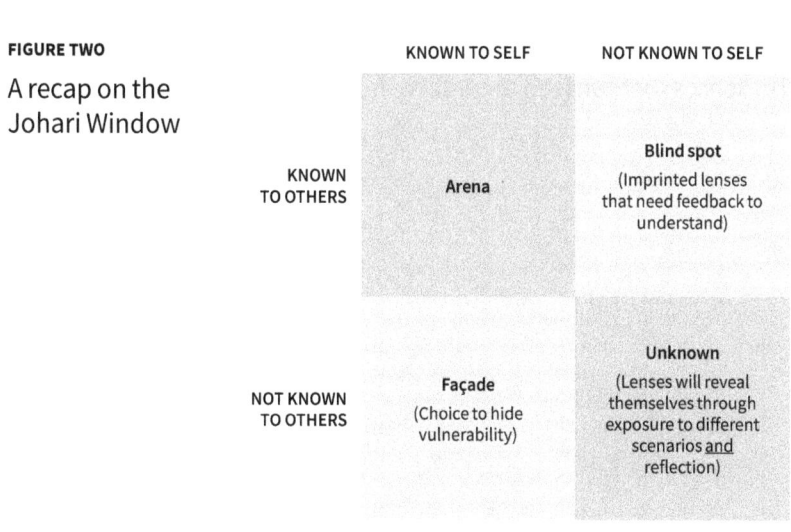

FIGURE TWO
A recap on the Johari Window

of this leads to growing elephants in the room, when not understood and honestly discussed.

People can also lack insight into their impact on others. The Johari Window* remains a useful model, (see Figure 2), to reflect on what people know about themselves. Things they are aware of, and things they aren't aware of. Unaddressed blind spots, create elephants.

So yes, it could be an individual who is your 'problem'. But only because they are experiencing the world differently to you and you aren't openly exploring this. It is useful to think about this concept as people seeing the world through different glasses. These glasses are made up of multiple lenses. We wear these lenses because of where we were born, the culture we grew up in, the experiences we have been exposed to. Each lens changes/distorts what we see in front of us. Therefore, how we view the world (see Figure 3).

---

* Psychologists Jonathon Luft and Harrington Ingham created the Johari Window in 1955.

FIGURE THREE

The lenses that can lead to conflict – how aware are you of your lenses?

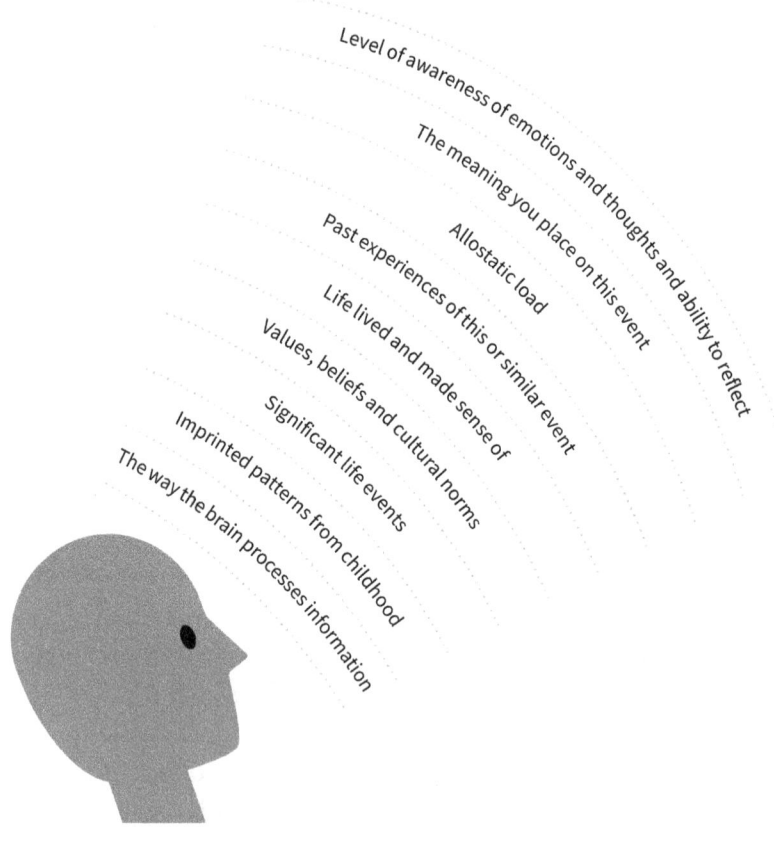

We are so used to wearing them, they can be invisible to us. So, when someone else has a completely different view/description of a situation, get curious on the lenses they are wearing, that are different to yours. Not being curious grows an elephant.

Use Table 1 to help you reflect on the individual that you find frustrating. Which of these lenses are contributing to the issue? What action could you take to stop the elephant from growing?

TABLE ONE
Practical initial steps to stop the elephant growing

The lenses that people are wearing that could be different to yours	Action to kick off to stop the elephant growing
Different styles of thinking.	How aware are you of your own style versus others? Do an assessment e.g. Business Chemistry by Deloitte with the whole team and discuss the implications of thinking differently. The reality of the tension it can create AND the benefit to problem solving that different perspectives bring.
Different ways of experiencing emotions. This can range from awareness of emotions in the first place, to intensity, and the ability to regulate them.	Accept that people do experience emotions differently. How emotionally literate are you? Start with improving your own literacy and regulation. Then introduce the concept to the team, so you can then use a common language to help everyone navigate the emotions of others more effectively.
Allostatic load – too much going on right now.	What is your allostatic load right now? Are you in the best place to support? What do they need right now? Time off? Redistribution of work? A regular sounding Board? Empathy from the team for not showing up at their best right now.
Mismatched/insufficient skills – they don't understand the world that they are operating in.	Can you teach them? Give them support to learn? Or are they best suited to a different role? Remember everyone has a 'zone of genius', you just need to help people find it sometimes.

The lenses that people are wearing that could be different to yours	Action to kick off to stop the elephant growing
Differing cultural heritage therefore acceptable practices/behaviour e.g. being deferential and not disagreeing, versus challenging authority. Direct vs indirect ways of talking.	This is a very broad topic. Being aware that there are natural differences is the start. Establish the connections across the team that helps you understand the cultural differences. Consider how you can work effectively in a way that embraces these differences rather than expecting them to change.
Perceived conflicting objectives.	Can you get them out on the table and find the common ground so people realise they don't conflict, and you can work together? Can you shift/realign objectives?
Blind Spots due to learned behaviour from prior experiences.	Yours or theirs? Interesting to ask yourself that question. Remind yourself 'everyone is doing the best they can with what they have'. When you assume good intent, it is easier to stay calm and given them feedback on their impact to help them learn. Remain open to the impact your blind spots may have.
Neurodivergence – the variety of ways people receive and process information	Help them feel safe and certain with you so you can explore the situation. What do they need you to do differently to help them process the information more effectively?

The team dynamic is the problem

The first team I ever led I absolutely loved. A small team, completely aligned with what we wanted to achieve. No real egos. An ability to have the conversations we needed to have. It was a dream. I didn't realise how good I had it until I moved from this to running a large department. I didn't know quite what had hit me. I discovered that my last team was the rarest of rare teams. They were a team comfortable with open dialogue but also a

FIGURE FOUR

The birth of the elephant – ignoring different perspectives

team that wore many similar lenses. Partly influenced by who they were as individuals and partly influenced by the alignment with environment. Landing a large department had me quickly assuming the team dynamic was 'the problem'.

It is not unreasonable to consider the dynamic of the team as 'the problem'. The reality is that every person comes to every situation wearing their unique lenses. Each of these shift the person's perspective. One person being 'the problem' is easy. Now you are multiplying this by everyone in the team. Elephants are born because each person experiences reality differently but assumes their reality is THE reality. Their reality is their reality. Each person will describe what is in front of them differently. Elephants grow when those different perspectives are not discussed openly and used constructively (Figure 4). When those different perspectives are continually not respected, quiet conflict becomes open, louder conflict.

Some may say conflict is a good thing in a team. Unchecked conflict, however, is as counterproductive as 'group think'. To be clear, there is a difference between creative conflict, where people deeply trust each other and welcome debate, versus social conflict that has people hiding or editing themselves. Creative conflict is valuable.

Embracing diversity of thought and ideas unlocks value.

Social conflict however shuts down people's willingness to express views. It keeps value under lock and key. Frustration with each other grows. People dig into the trench of being right. The elephant continues to grow. The more you can get your teams to understand and respect the value that different lenses bring, the less unhelpful social conflict and the more helpful creative conflict there is.

Again, as with the individual, it is not unreasonable to think that the team dynamic is 'the problem'. Not talking about this dynamic is a greater problem, which grows an elephant. They key message to your team members then, is to stay curious. When they feel that tension arising in them because of how others are behaving, get them to check in with their own stories in their heads. See if they can intentionally work to understand someone else's perspective. Remember, when you can collectively see the full 3D elephant, from all its angles, it shrinks. When you keep ignoring or not respecting, different perspectives, the elephant grows to the point of conflict.

It's the system and processes that are the problem

While it is perfectly reasonable to consider people as 'the problem', it is also reasonable for you to turn to the way in which the organisation operates as 'the problem'. Figure 5 represents layers of the ecosystem you are operating within. These layers include:
- The culture and sub-culture of teams.
- How your IT, Finance, People and Culture, Risk Management systems and processes work.
- The business objectives.
- The market pressures.
- How work is designed.

The workplace is an ecosystem. A complex organism with many moving parts. It is constantly working to maintain balance. It can seem impossible to change. Not talking about the reality of these challenges and making changes, grows elephants. Reflect on the ecosystem you work in. Where might the elephants exist?

How many of the following scenarios have you experienced?
- Lack of alignment in objectives (particularly when tied to incentives), which has teams looking after their own interests.
- A culture of always making sure objectives linked to incentives are hit. Even if the behaviour required to achieve these objectives, isn't aligned with the organisation's stated values.
- Workload distribution not being equal.
- Two departments continually saying the other is responsible for resolving an issue.
- External market pressures resulting in unsustainable pressure to deliver.

What a truck load of elephants there potentially are in a workplace ecosystem! No wonder conflict is inevitable when you

FIGURE FIVE

An entire eco-system of potential conflict – elephants in every layer. Where do the elephants exist for you?

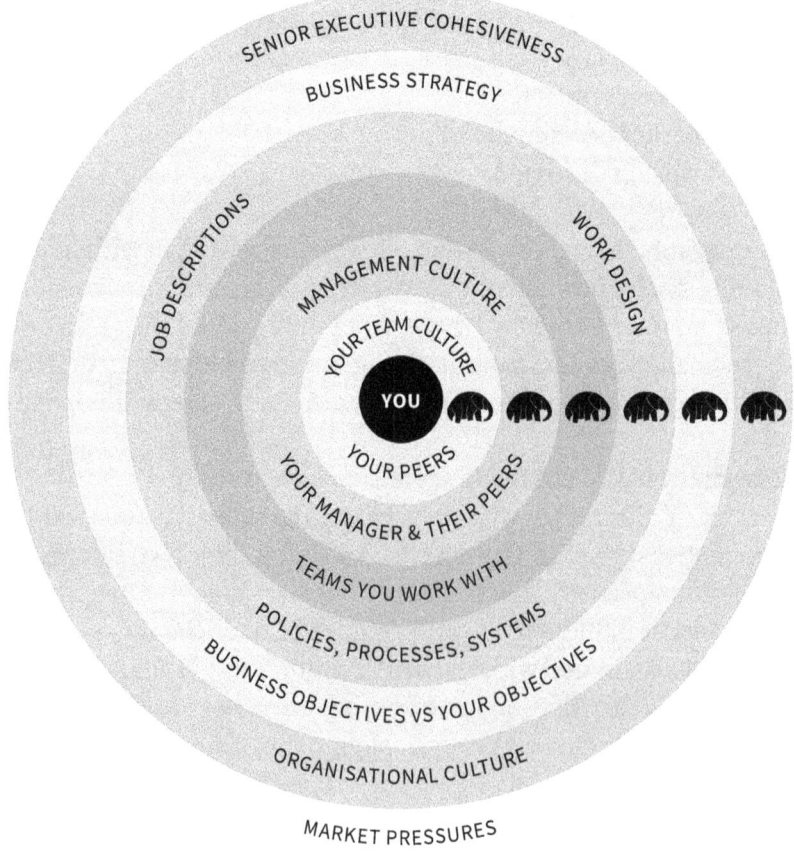

think about how all these layers interact and what people don't talk about.

Each layer can create different elephants. All these layers together set people up for potential conflict. When you then add in the lenses each individual wears, then we are talking a herd of elephants. It can feel hard sometimes to get work done in an ecosystem full of elephants.

There are many people who just shrug and accept this ecosystem. They put their head in the sand. Or become that bull in a china shop. Pushing their way through, to get what they want. This is where an organisation doesn't reach its potential. Value is locked in by the elephants.

When you are part of a large ecosystem, it can be hard to see what you can influence in these macro issues. The starting point is believing you can have an impact. Identify what you can do within your own area with regards to the Five Cs of accountability. Which peers have enough insight for you to get them on board, to do this too? We will return later in this book to larger scale skill building in elephant shrinking that really shifts entire ecosystems. If you want to start influencing the ecosystem though, you need to get curious about where the elephants are.

Ouch…is it me? Do I create elephants?

Have you ever done that exercise in a large group where you are asked what percentage of drivers are bad drivers? Then asked to put your hand up if you are a good driver and everyone puts their hand up? What a miracle! There are no bad drivers in the room. But really?

I thought I was an inclusive leader. I valued everyone's opinion and welcomed everyone. It wasn't until I was faced with the realisation that I had a transgender son, that I appreciated something

I was blind to. I had no lived experience in this space. My lens of the trans community was created through what I had experienced to date. Which was limited to inaccurate portrayals in movies (as I realised when I watched Disclosure* with my son). Supporting and loving my son, and subsequently being an executive sponsor for Pride, created a whole new lens for me. One which understood people's natural fear, discomfort and reactions, when they didn't have lived experience. When they relied on their understanding, from misinformed media. I had a blind spot. From lived experience, I now wear a different lens. One which I would like to think, brings empathy and understanding to people feeling uncomfortable about unfamiliar situations. Being curious to what I could learn about myself through this new experience, has removed a blind spot that could create elephants and helped me be a better leader.

The more successful you have been in climbing the ladder with a particular approach though, the greater the risk that you become convinced, that the way you view the world is right. The higher up you go in an organisation, the greater the impact also of your blind spots on others. The greater the risk, that you yourself are creating elephants (Figure 6).

'We are literally perceptually blind to systems that exist outside our mental model of the way the world works.'†

Everyone has their own perspectives because of their deeply imprinted lenses. Everyone can get caught in feeling that their view is right and there is no elephant. You are no different. You have had a way of operating, imprinted in you from your genetics/culture/early childhood. Reinforced through how you have

---
* Netflix movie helping people understand the distorted view of transgender people that movies had been providing
† Siegel, D.J. MD. (2022) Intraconnected: Mwe (Me + We) as the Integration of Self, Identity and Belonging. Norton agency titles. New York. USA.

FIGURE SIX

Your words/actions get amplified in meaning and can be distorted the higher you go in an organisation

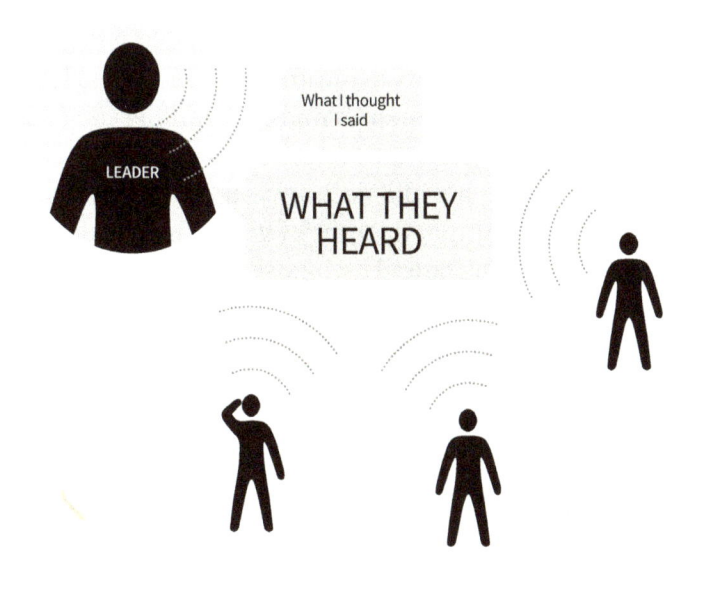

navigated the world to date. It is neither a wrong nor right way to view the world. It is purely **your** way of viewing the world. The lenses you wear, create your unique blind spots. Not accepting and getting curious about these can create elephants, when you interact with others. The question is, do you want that to change?

Why change? The economic principle of trust[*] is that a high level of trust equals a low cost of doing business. A low level of trust equals a high cost of doing business. Blind spots interfere with building deep trust. That is why you want to change.

---

[*] Covey S.M.R. with Merrill, R.R. (2012). The speed of trust: The One Thing That Changes Everything. Simon & Schuster, UK.

Change firstly lies in you becoming more aware of the lenses you wear. Some of those lenses will be very hard to remove. Knowing they exist however, can allow you to recognise when a particular lens will provide a different view of the world to others. From there you can then choose how you want to respond to the situations you are faced with. The good news is that when you are faced with significant events in life and you are open to learning, you will find those lenses keep changing. Enabling you to take in a broader view of the elephant, faster.

Learning to pause and choose how you show up at any point in time is the opportunity in front of you. It helps you to avoid elephants in the first place and recognise them quickly when they appear. Your ability to become more self-aware, to regulate your emotions and thoughts, to choose helpful responses, is where it all starts.

> *'Between stimulus and response there is a space. In that space is our power to choose our response. In our response lies our growth and our freedom.'**

Your role as a leader, is to stay calm, connected, curious, and caring in the moment. This is most definitely easier said than done. Accessing that space is critical. Under pressure, what behaviour most commonly shows up in you?

> *When you stay calm, connected, curious, and caring with someone else, you have the best opportunity to help them feel seen, heard, and that they matter.*

This helps them to stay/become calm, to then get curious. Curiosity from involved parties, shrinks the elephant. But you will

---

* Frankl V.E. (2004). Man's search for Meaning: The classic tribute to hope from the Holocaust. Ebury Publishing, Random House Group. UK.

not be able to be this all the time. Those lenses you wear, your own allostatic load, and the environment you are operating in, will cause unwanted emotions and stories to bubble up for you at inconvenient times. This can be so uncomfortable. But ignore your blind spots and therefore growth at your own peril. You do not want to be a major contributor to elephants in your organisation. Learning to recognise when your behaviour hasn't been helpful and understanding what is driving this, helps you learn more about your lenses. Understanding your lenses, helps you see the elephants.

PRACTICAL STEPS:

Becoming curious about yourself and your lenses

When you find yourself getting tense/annoyed/frustrated/irritated/confused by others, instead of going straight to the assumption that they are the problem, ask yourself:

- What emotion are you feeling right now? Label it. And breathe through it first to decrease its intensity. Your ability to become aware faster of what emotions are coming up is step number one in not contributing to conflict unnecessarily.
- What's the story inside your head about the situation/the person?
- What might be a different explanation? That is, how can you take their perspective for a moment. Assuming good intent on their behalf, how might your lenses be different to theirs?
- Can you use a few slow, deep breaths and remain curious in conversation with them, to learn more about their lenses as well as yours?

The more you do this, the more you can identify what stories come up more often for you. This helps you recognise lenses you are wearing.

Key things to remember

People wear multiple lenses that influence their perspective on the world.

Not talking about them, grows unwieldy big elephants that cause conflict. Talking about the different perspectives openly, shrinks elephants to unlocks people's potential.

Lack of accountability, in one or more people, that isn't addressed, is a primary cause of elephants in organisations. People hold themselves accountable at work because you have put the Five Cs into play.

1. **Clarity**: Have you been clear on what you need them to do and how it relates to/impacts on what others are doing?
2. **Capability**: Have you recruited for the right skills for this job?
3. **Capacity**: Have you provided them with enough time/resources?
4. **Coaching**: Are you encouraging them, in a safe environment, through curious questions?
5. **Consequences**: Are you measuring them objectively on what they do? Recognising them for delivering or being clear on where you need change? Are you supporting them, so they understand the guardrails they are operating between, feeling encouraged and energised?

Beyond the Five Cs, people may contribute to a growing elephant because:
- They think/process differently to most of the group and this isn't accepted.
- They have other issues going on for them that they don't feel comfortable talking about (allostatic load).
- They have blind spots that can lead to dysfunctional ways of dealing with issues.
- Their own cultural influences, their heritage and/or the culture of workplace reinforces ways of dealing with conflict.

When you layer accountability with the perceptions that each person brings to the table and the ecosystem of the organisation, it is clear why conflict is inevitable. **Everyone is trying to make sense of the world, and in doing so, can become easily convinced**

they have THE right perspective. Multiple 'right' perspectives, that aren't accepted, create big elephants.

You can now see how elephants can easily form and grow when left unchecked. In the next chapter I will take you inside the human brain. Don't worry, I won't get you caught up in lots of medical jargon. I do believe however, that some basic science helps you make sense of how our brains create the lenses that can distort our perspective of the elephant. Once you understand this, you can then move on to how you might start practically learning about different perspectives of the elephant, rather than run for the hills.

In the meantime, stay curious. Observe yourself and others when unhelpful emotions bubble up and consider:
- What is the story inside your head right now?
- How might that be contributing to a growing elephant?

CHAPTER TWO

HOW YOUR BRAIN GROWS ELEPHANTS

Having been introduced to the lenses that distort people's views of the elephant, it is useful to explore some science on how the brain operates, that creates these lenses. Do not be alarmed though. This isn't a scientific book. I promise it won't get too technical. It is however useful for you to anchor your decisions in shrinking elephants in science. The science is the secret sauce.

To help you grasp this secret sauce, I will take you through three areas in this chapter:
- Why your brain constantly looks for patterns, threats and connection, and what chemicals get released when your brain experiences these things.
- The mental and physical health continuum that everyone moves around on.
- Psychological safety, and its role in unlocking innovation.

How your brain operates

The simplest way of thinking about your brain, is that it is divided into two parts. Your thinking brain, and your animal brain. (It is a bit more complicated, but this is a useful way of understanding it for the purpose of shrinking elephants). The animal brain is the part of the brain that you aren't usually consciously aware of. It is doing things without your cognitive control. Things like breathing, sweating, digesting, blinking, growing hair. Your animal brain is fundamentally wired for your survival.

One of the animal brain's primary functions is to constantly scan the environment seeking for patterns. Pattern is how the brain makes sense of the world. It enables the brain to filter the information that is coming at it, from all that is going on in the environment, so you don't get overwhelmed. It will deem certain patterns as safe to be ignored. It has seen the pattern before. The pattern makes sense and is safe. It has also learnt certain patterns are potential threats.

Patterns become the stories that the brain has hard wired in to keep you alive.

In this constant scanning for patterns, what is identified as different is first perceived as a potential threat. Be it physical or psychological. To help you respond to that 'threat', the animal brain releases cortisol. This picks up your heart rate. It puts you on alert. It gets you ready for whatever immediate action is appropriate, to keep you safe. When faced with a perceived threat, the action might be to run away from the threat (flight); to turn and face the threat head on (fight); become the proverbial deer in headlights and not take any action (freeze) or try and 'please' the attacker i.e. so they don't see you as a threat (fawn).

'To speed up processing time so we can move toward the safety of predictability, our brain often makes snap judgements, distorting or misrepresenting the available information.'[*]

The brain wants you to respond quickly. The response you automatically take, when you feel that cortisol rush, often follows a learnt pattern. Some people have learnt from early childhood that avoidance is the best option. Others always face it, but aggressively. (That is, 'attack is the best form of defence' mode.) Others will get stuck in the freeze mode, caught in fear, not knowing what to do with it. And others turn to pleasing their perceived threat, to stay safe. The point is, while the cortisol plays an incredibly important role in helping you to act, the learnt pattern of response is not always the most useful response.

When you experience someone else 'attacking' you, avoiding you, not listening to you, or constantly trying to please you, this is them doing the best they can with what they have, a brain flooded with cortisol.

It is easy to lay blame at their feet, as the one with 'the problem'. They are not necessarily seeing the world clearly. But this isn't a useful response from you, when you want to deliver value in your organisation. While unchecked cortisol grows the elephant, there are three chemicals, when all present, that help you decrease the cortisol, to then be capable of shrinking the elephant.

The three key chemicals for shrinking elephants are oxytocin, serotonin, and dopamine. If you want someone to feel more connected, able to listen fully and solve complex problems, they need to have all three chemicals triggered. First, they need to feel

---

[*] Le Pera, N. Dr (2023), How to Be the Love you Seek: Break Cycles, Find Peace and Heal your relationships. Harper Wave. USA.

like they belong. When they feel like they are part of a tribe, they feel safe, and oxytocin floods their brain. They need more than just feeling like they belong though to help shrink elephants. They need to feel that they play a valuable role in this tribe. When they feel valued for their contribution, their brains get a hit of serotonin. Both these chemicals help the person see a pattern of safety, not threat. When they can get this, they are more able to get curious with you on how to best understand the emerging elephant. Getting a healthy dopamine hit. Table 2 summarises these important balancing chemicals.

When you get a good balance of oxytocin, serotonin, and dopamine, then you balance out the cortisol enough to see the elephant through different eyes.

In many workplaces/teams, there is not enough oxytocin and serotonin. People see they are only really valued if they deliver the desired result. Therefore, they focus on achievement alone. Getting dopamine hits for achievement is like a sugar rush. It feels great, then it fades. You need the next achievement to keep offsetting the cortisol. You then don't feel safe. Except in those moments of achievement. You are running on a hamster wheel. With high cortisol and only dopamine to offset it, people become hyper aware of differences. They can start seeing patterns in what others would see are very neutral situations. This hyper aware mode grows the elephant. This is not conducive to long term health or performance.

Empathy for how uncertainty increases cortisol and recognising how to help trigger oxytocin and serotonin in others, is critical to your ability to shrink elephants.

You can start learning more about these chemicals through paying attention to your own reactions. Become aware of when

TABLE TWO

The chemicals we need in balance in our brain to contribute to shrinking elephants

Brain Chemical	How it gets triggered	Role
Cortisol	Something different or a pattern that your brain recognises has caused issues in the past therefore likely will again.	Alerts us to danger and pushes us to action – fight/flight/fawn (please others) and freeze (not sure what to do).
Oxytocin	Hugs, laughter, getting support, doing things together in a group. That sense of belonging.	Calms us down and helps us feel safe.
Serotonin	When you help others. When your skills are valued by others. Through positive feedback.	Helps us feel good about ourselves/happy.
Dopamine	Learning new patterns. Achieving a goal. Solving a problem. Can become an addiction if this is the only chemical used to offset the cortisol. E.g. social media, gambling.	Food for the brain, helps us enjoy learning and makes us feel awesome as a reward when we work out a new pattern.

you find your heart racing; or muscles tensing; or breathing becoming that bit shallower. Become aware of any intense emotion, that may or may not seem out of kilter with the situation you face. Somehow your brain has identified something isn't quite right. What is it? What is the story that is in your head about the situation? Can you take a deep breath and see a different perspective? The more you can become aware of your cortisol response and breathe slowly before you respond, the better you will become as an elephant shrinker and therefore leader.

The health continuums

Your physical and mental health moves along a continuum. From great (green), to average (yellow), to not great (orange) to seriously not great (red). Figures 7 and 8, reproduced from Mentally at Work[*], give you a summary of what's happening at each point in the continuum. Your health is never static. Your lifestyle choices and allostatic load, heavily influence where you are at any one point in time.

Where people are at on the health continuums will influence their view of the elephant and therefore their response to conflict.

Be aware that the more you remain in yellow, verging on orange, the greater the risk that yellow becomes your new 'green'. That is, you have normalised feeling slightly on edge. This is a danger to both your physical and mental health. Your body is not designed to have constant cortisol spikes without relief.

Have you ever found that tension in the body/intense annoyance and perhaps saying something that you regret (or when in private swearing your head off) when:
- Someone in your household has left the place messy.
- The bins didn't go out.
- Someone doesn't deliver when they said they would.
- You get criticised in a meeting.
- Someone cuts you off in traffic.
- You lose power right when you are working on submitting a key piece of work.

---

[*] Hawkins, G. (2020). Mentally at Work: Optimising health and business performance through connection. Mentally at Work. Melbourne, Australia.

Remember the concept of the last straw that broke the camel's back? This over reaction is you having accepted sitting in yellow for an extended period.

Your reaction to a situation gives insight into where you are on the continuum.

You will never stay in green all the time. None of us do, physically or mentally. You can however get better at becoming aware of where you are on the continuum at any point in time, actively choosing to do things that get you back to green. Through consciously seeking those balancing chemicals. It is important in reading this, if you recognise yourself as perhaps being in the orange or even the red, that you seek professional help. In those moments when you find it hard to steady yourself, the anchor of others is critical.

Take a moment to reflect on the information in Figures 7 and 8 and your own health right now:
- What colour would you use to describe your physical and mental health?
- What practical actions might you take to improve your health?

I encourage you to introduce these continuums and the language of the colours, to your team.

Sharing a common language plays an important part in triggering a feeling of belonging and therefore oxytocin. It enables you to fast-track problem solving as you are coming from a more solid base of feeling connected in a common language.

For example, a team member being able to say 'hey I am having a bit of a yellow day today' is a simple way of letting others in

FIGURE SEVEN

The continuum of physical health

THE PHYSICAL HEALTH CONTINUUM

GREEN	YELLOW	ORANGE	RED
Consistent balanced diet	Not eating well	Consistent unbalanced diet	Severe physical illness needing clinical care to improve/manage
Regular exercise	Not exercising for a short period	Overweight and/or very unfit – breathless in day to day activities	Ability to reliably hold down full-time work and perform is compromised either short term or long term
Sleeping well	Restless nights without sleeping		
Reasonably good energy levels	Binge eating or heavy drinking	Minor injuries – a muscle tear, continually ill with minor issues	
	Obsessing about diets		Treatment starts outside the inpatient stay but at the seriously dark red end, people are hospitalised and ultimately the darkest of the red is life threatening

| GREEN | YELLOW | ORANGE | RED |

FIGURE EIGHT

The continuum of psychological health

THE PSYCHOLOGICAL HEALTH CONTINUUM

GREEN	YELLOW	ORANGE	RED
A range of good emotions but overall feeling balanced and broadly in control	Feeling unbalanced /flat or frustrated, annoyed, irritated	Weeks of persistent flat or down moods that are starting to interfere with relationships	Severe mental illness needing clinical care to improve/manage
Experiencing joy and happiness at times but also contentment and high engagement	Angry beyond the actual conversation	Mild anxiety – heart palpitations	The ability to reliably hold down full-time work and perform is compromised either short term or long term
	Not sleeping well, not eating well, not exercising	Worried most of the time about a range of issues	
Feel like you belong	Can't stop thinking about a particular issue	Allowing emotions to dictate responses to situations with responses out of proportion to actual events	Treatment starts outside the inpatient stay but at the seriously dark red end, people are hospitalised and ultimately the darkest of the red is life threatening

| GREEN | YELLOW | ORANGE | RED |

the team know they aren't absolutely 100%. This can help the team choose their response. To help that person feel like they belong, are valued and they will be supported to get the work done. Common language allows support to come faster.

Do you feel psychologically safe?

Psychological safety, defined by Amy Edmondson, who is at the forefront of research in this area is:

> 'A belief that one will not be punished or humiliated for speaking up with ideas, questions, concerns, or mistakes, and that the team is safe for interpersonal risk.'[*]

The negative experience of feeling psychologically unsafe 'disrupts and derails thinking, and emotions, damages relationships, impacts productivity, and damages health… research shows that a "hit" to our psychological safety can have a deeper and longer-lasting impact than a "hit" to our physical selves'.[†] Indeed, it is this potential for the harm to health that has driven legislation to protect employees.

> 'The absence of psychological safety can inflict devastating emotional wounds, neutralise performance, paralyse potential and crater an

---

[*] Edmonson, A. (2012). Teaming: How Organizations Learn, Innovate, and Compete in the Knowledge Economy. John Wiley & Sons Inc. San Francisco, CA, USA.

[†] Radecki, D. PhD, MA & Hull, L. (2021). Psychological Safety: The key to happy, high-performing people and teams. The Academy of Brain-based Leadership, Red Hill Publishing. California, USA.

individual's sense of self-worth. The implication is that organisations that lack psychological safety are galloping their way to extinction'[*]

Given the implications the research is indicating, you clearly would want an environment that is always safe, to protect health AND get better outcomes. The question is, is this an unreachable nirvana when you know how the brain operates?

Psychological safety can be complex. Legislation focuses on the employer obligations. It is reasonable that you take responsibility as a leader to create a healthy, safe environment for your teams. This is in both yours and all team members' interests.

The challenge with the employer obligations is that it doesn't adequately consider the reality that every single person comes to their interactions with their unique set of lenses:
- Their own trauma – past and recent.
- Unconscious ways of operating that have worked for them to survive to date but may not be helpful in this situation.
- Their own values, and therefore beliefs, in how others should behave toward them.
- Their own level of cortisol due to the allostatic load of their life at any point in time.
- Their own ability (or lack thereof) to be able to talk to others about how they are feeling.

'True physical and emotional safety and security begins in our body, and until we can feel this safety and security within ourselves, we can't feel safe and secure with others.'[†]

---

[*] Clark, T.R. (2020) The 4 Stages of Psychological Safety: Defining the Path to Inclusion and Innovation. Berrett-Koehler Publishers Inc. California, USA.

[†] Le Pera, N. Dr (2023), How to Be the Love you Seek: Break Cycles, Find Peace and Heal your relationships. Harper Wave. USA.

All these factors influence how people interpret each other's behaviour. Psychological safety is hard to achieve, for everyone, always, when people wear very different lenses. Seeing the elephant from very different perspectives.

Clark's model of psychological safety identifies four stages, providing greater nuance to what it looks like. Each stage builds on the one prior. I like the depth of Clark's stages. It helps people see that there are precursors that need to be present before you can get to the penultimate definition of psychological safety. (The ability to raise concerns without fear of the consequences.) There is a clear link between what Clark is proposing as the four stages, and the chemicals that are in our brain when we experience these (see Table 3).

It is important to recognise, even in the best environments, not everyone will feel psychologically safe all the time. If there are restructures and retrenchments, people won't feel safe. If someone is being performance managed, they won't feel safe. This feeling of safety needs to be treated in a similar continuum to that for our health. It is ok and normal to go into yellow and not feel safe. The question is, do you have enough awareness to recognise this? Then take action to get back to green. Psychological safety isn't feeling 'safe' all the time per se. It is knowing, even when you don't feel safe (a cortisol burst), that you can raise concerns about this, and you will be heard. In a psychologically safe workplace, you will continue to have moments of feeling 'unsafe', but they aren't sustained because the leaders appreciate the lenses that create elephants and respond with connection and curiosity. Leaders may not always respond effectively though, due to the complication of their own lenses.

Do you feel safe at work right now? Building on the understanding of the continuum of health already discussed, Table 4 can help you identify at any point in time, where you are on the continuum of safety and what you might do to bring yourself, (or someone

TABLE THREE

Clark's 4 stages of psychological safety and the link to our animal brain

Clark's 4 Stages	Emotions/Thoughts	Chemical triggered
1. Inclusion safety	I feel like I belong	Oxytocin triggered and the person relaxes
2. Learner safety	I feel supported to learn the environment/tasks/skills. It feels good to learn new things.	The early dopamine of interesting learning
3. Contributor safety	I feel recognised and valued for what I bring to the organisation and therefore feel safe to bring my best self to work in what I do. I then feel energized to contribute more	The regular hits of serotonin
4. Challenger safety	I feel safe to raise issues and concerns without fear of negative consequences. This is the brain picking up patterns of concern (cortisol hit), but the person can stay curious and raise the questions, because of the layers below building their safety and therefore trust and confidence in their leaders.	Short burst of cortisol then a combination of all three chemicals. Oxytocin from belonging to a tribe that they know behaves in this way. Serotonin for feeling valued for raising the issue. Dopamine in helping to solve it.

else), back to green. The continuum of safety highlights you will naturally slide into the yellow zone. You may occasionally hit the orange zone. You want to identify this quickly though, to avoid sliding into the red zone.

People will not naturally feel safe all the time. There is a significant difference though, between feeling that discomfort fleetingly as you dip into the yellow versus it being sustained over a period, significantly impacting people's health and the business's outcomes. When people don't feel safe, the elephant grows. Leaders who are emotionally detached, focused on preserving their own reputation above supporting their own team and their peers around them, will not create the right environment for the organisation to sustainably perform. These leaders do not make it safe. These leaders create a fear-based environment.

> *'Relationships are at the heart of everything and the antidote to fear.'**

Your role as a leader is to take practical steps to build your relationships with your team, to extend the amount of time people are in the green, feeling safe.

---

* Grange, P. Dr (2021) Fear Less: How to win at life without losing yourself. Vermilion. UK.

TABLE FOUR

How safe are you feeling? The Psychological Safety Continuum

How you might be feeling/thinking			
I feel like I am seen for who I am; I am heard and understood, and I matter. I feel calm/balanced and can bring my best self to the table.	'Ouch' that hurt. Gee that person/people annoys/irritates me. I feel unbalanced/not quite right. A moment of discomfort.	I don't feel like that person/people understand what I am going through. Why can't the other person see that they did the wrong thing/aren't making it easy for me? When I see them, I feel those emotions bubbling up again. I don't trust them. Running on adrenalin, determined to achieve. I think I am ok, but I have built an exoskeleton of tension and momentum around me to avoid feeling/thinking about uncomfortable situations or relationships.	I feel so angry/hurt. That person/people only cares about themselves. They have no right to treat me this way. I am really struggling, and they don't seem to care at all. I don't know how I can continue to work in this environment. There is too much work. I don't have enough control or clarity, and no one is giving me constructive feedback to help me.
GREEN	**YELLOW**	**ORANGE**	**RED**

THE PSYCHOLOGICAL SAFETY CONTINUUM

How might it show up?

GREEN	YELLOW	ORANGE	RED
Fully present in the moment.	Slightly distracted/ not fully present to the next situation.	Negative stories and feelings about a person/situation seem to keep popping up again and again in your head leading you to seek emotional reinforcement (consciously or unconsciously) from others on being right.	Not sleeping well.
Good at listening to others.	Heart rate increases.		Making poor choices with food/drink.
Energy for the work being done.	Breathing may get shallower.		Constantly seeking distraction.
Able to hold your own boundaries on what's important to you.		The thoughts/feelings get in the way of the job focus. You find yourself being much shorter/more abrupt with others.	Escalated feelings interfere with the ability to get work done and others are noticing that.
Steady heart rate and breathing.			Emotional outburst, withdrawal, chronic sickness, feeling overwhelmed.
		If running on adrenalin, the tension builds physically and psychologically. You may experience headaches/body pains.	Vicious cycle of hyper vigilance to threat and seeing patterns of threat that aren't always there.

What's happening in your nervous system?

GREEN	YELLOW	ORANGE	RED
Good balance of the chemicals. The brain can focus, learn, and solve problems.	Cortisol has spiked briefly. Your body reacts quickly, wanting you to manage the 'threat'. The classic fight, flight, freeze or fawn response.	Cortisol hasn't gone down quickly. The system is over stimulated with cortisol and needs a stronger dose of those balancing chemicals to get it back to green.	Chronic levels of cortisol not reducing. Getting hooked on addictive behaviours to manage the cortisol. A belief that achieving things (I'll be happy when…) is the way out. Dopamine hits keep the body going until it can't anymore. Illness then takes over.

GREEN → YELLOW → ORANGE → RED

THE PSYCHOLOGICAL SAFETY CONTINUUM

What might be needed in that moment/situation?

GREEN	YELLOW	ORANGE	RED
Savour and enjoy the moment. ___ Stay present, focused on connection, contribution and curiosity.	Take a slow, deep breath, recognising the cortisol has spiked. This may be enough. Otherwise get curious. What is your brain detecting as a threat? Can you shake it off literally by shaking your arms/legs, doing some star jumps or going for a walk? i.e. allowing the emotion triggered by the cortisol to flush out of your body, as it recognises it is safe. ___ Journal on what has happened. What story are you telling yourself? Is that helpful? Is there a more helpful story?	Consciously reach out for oxytocin from your support network. Focus on doing things that you are good at. Help other people, to get some serotonin. You just need a bit more of a 'hit' than usual to offset the increased cortisol. This enables you to start getting curious about what stories are in your head and how you might re-shape them.	There will be a range of things needed here, some of which are contained in this book. The first step is recognising you need help. Who is in your support network who you trust to help you with implementing the strategies from the orange section? You may feel like avoiding it at this point, but that will only make it worse. Support is needed. Please get it.

What could you do if you recognise this state in someone else?

GREEN	YELLOW	ORANGE	RED
Enjoy it with them. ___ Maximise it, focusing on working together on the hard stuff.	You will likely only be aware if they tell you. ___ Listen fully if they tell you. Thank them for sharing it. Acknowledge the story and the emotion. Check if they can breathe through it and shake it off. Go for a walk around the block with them (you can do this virtually by both walking while on the phone to each other), to help them shake it off.	Build on the yellow techniques. Help them get curious. Proactively reach out with 'I couldn't help but notice in that last meeting…' ___ Listen to their story. Ask them, how is it helping you? What's a more useful story? ___ How do you trigger oxytocin and serotonin in them by having them feel connected to and valued by you.	Performance is usually impacted here but don't start with performance. Start with the person. Put time aside to help them. ___ Reflect on how you have interacted with them. How you consistently keep triggering oxytocin and serotonin in them to help them get through it.

GREEN YELLOW ORANGE RED →

THE PSYCHOLOGICAL SAFETY CONTINUUM

Key things to remember

In this chapter you have explored...

Some basics in how ALL brains work:
- **We are all wired to look for patterns** (or lack thereof) that may indicate threats, that tell us whether we are safe or not.
- **We are all wired to belong** – we are tribal by nature.
- **When we feel threatened, cortisol spikes.**
- Feeling like we belong, valued and learning, helps to balance out the cortisol, allowing us to focus and perform.

Your role as a leader in helping your team experience a healthy balance between:
- **Cortisol** – to get them **hyper-focused** in those challenging moments.
- **Oxytocin** – so they can relax into **feeling like they belong**, bringing their genuine best self to work.
- **Serotonin** – so they **feel valued** enough to keep contributing.
- **Dopamine** – so they can **curiously help solve** the problems the organisation faces.

Psychological safety as the foundation for performance:
- People can move in and out of this safety on a continuum.
- How safe do you feel right now? From green, to yellow, to orange, to red?

This chapter has been all about starting to tune into how your brain functions. The more you become familiar with how to influence these chemicals, the more effective you will be at creating the optimal environment. Enabling cohesive teams to deliver amazing results. I encourage you to introduce this common language to your teams, so everyone can become more aware of how the animal brain responds to the situations it detects. Whilst it has only been a basic introduction to the brain, once you start to understand how the brain works, where relationship conflict comes from starts to make sense. In this next chapter, I'll dive deeper with you into some of the nuances of the common lenses you may find in the workplace and how to work with them, to shrink elephants.

CHAPTER THREE

SPOTTING COMMON ELEPHANTS

My wise mother would often remind me:
'People are doing the best they can with what they have.'

This was a common response from her at the dinner table, when I would express frustration with someone in my team. The person who seems to be oversensitive; always complaining; always believing they are right; always suggesting a different answer, seemingly for the sake of it.

We are uniquely us in every situation. Certain aspects of us are amplified or dulled down, depending on how our brains are perceiving the environment and how our lenses interact with another person, at any point in time. However, I want to show you some of the more common behaviour patterns I have experienced that can grow elephants when not addressed, and how you might get curious about what is driving them. This should start you thinking about the uniqueness of the lenses people wear.

In our uniqueness however, we need to remember what we have in common:
- We are all wired to survive. Our animal brain will never stop looking for pattern to make meaning.
- We all have our own deep-rooted stories, behaviours and related emotions, with varying insight into the impact these have on others.
- We all have varying degrees of willingness and comfort to face our past in a curious way. This is heavily influenced by our current level of awareness, and how much benefit our brain sees it gets from sticking with its known responses.
- We all live in autopilot for a significant proportion of our day (otherwise we would be exhausted/overwhelmed all the time).
- People's automatic unhelpful reactions to others that cause conflict, come from an animal brain level of fear that they may not be aware of.

Within that context, I want to explore the following:
- The Five Steps to establishing connection with your team.
- Working with common behaviours seen in the workplace.
- Ill health and Workers' Compensation. How this can create a downward spiral of conflict.
- Appreciating your own deeply ingrained lenses
- The nuances to consider when you are caught with an elephant between you and a peer or manager.

Where does connection with others start?

20% of your team, will take up 80% of your energy because they wear significantly different lenses to you.

When you can have diversity of perspectives around the table, the questions you can ask each other can generate great insights. To bring our best curiosity to the table to solve problems though, we need to feel that we are seen, we are heard and that we matter. Our ability to connect and therefore trust each other is the starting point to openly accept and explore different angles of the elephant.

Never underestimate the power of finding that thing in common with someone else as a strong foundation for being able to explore different perspectives. I remember going into my first meeting with a partner for a global consulting company as we were about to kick off a major project with them. While they were ready, with the Program Director, to talk about their approach to the project, I asked them to pause and spend ten minutes with me working out what we had in common that had nothing to do with work. I explained to them my expectations that things would go wrong in the project. Having strong connection between us would help us build the trusted bond, to make those difficult conversations easier. The partner and I discovered we were both one of nine children! We found immediate respect for each other in navigating such an environment. We had the inevitable challenges I expected to have in the project. The bond of being one of nine though, made the difference in enabling us to talk openly and explore options for resolution together.

FIGURE NINE

Do you see me? The 5 steps to better connection

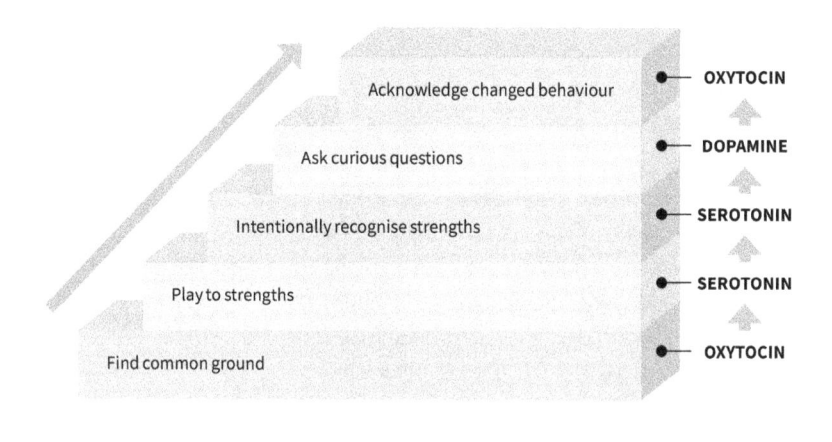

Step	Neurochemical
Acknowledge changed behaviour	OXYTOCIN
Ask curious questions	DOPAMINE
Intentionally recognise strengths	SEROTONIN
Play to strengths	SEROTONIN
Find common ground	OXYTOCIN

If you want to keep elephants to a minimum, it starts with you making sure the people you work with, feel seen by you. Connection is the foundation for trust that enables differences to be explored with curiosity.

There are five steps to establish this connection. This connection enables people to feel seen. It builds trust (Figure 9).

PRACTICAL STEPS:

Do you see me? Implementing the Five Steps to better connection

The starting point for all teams, regardless of who you have in them, is to develop connection and therefore trust between people. To do this, use the Five Steps to connection to help them feel seen, valued and that they matter.

1. **Find common ground: Find out what you have in common** with them that has nothing to do with work and bring that into conversation regularly. Not for long conversations, but a reminder. Oxytocin gets elicited when we feel like we belong. It could be a sporting team (but don't assume this because some people have learnt to look enthusiastic about sport to fit in). It could be theatre, a genre of films or books, type of pet, a type of exercise, cooking, eating out, comedy or a particular hobby.

2. **Play to strengths: Observe to find out where their strengths lie.** Can you influence what they do for them to play to their strengths? This helps to elicit serotonin.

3. **Intentionally recognise strengths: Reflect** on how you **recognise** their strengths and thank them for it, publicly and privately. Again, eliciting serotonin.

4. **Ask Curious Questions: How do you help them get curious** (eliciting dopamine as they get an 'ah ha' moment and feelings of achievement)? Ask great questions of them. Questions that get them learning about themselves and contributing more fully.

5. **Acknowledge changed behaviour: Observe for changes in their behaviour.** If they have responded in a way that seems out of character, check in with them to acknowledge the change and find out what you can do to support. This elicits further oxytocin by feeling seen and cared for. When someone is struggling, another person (be it manager or peer), recognising that and helping them talk through it, will go a long way to a faster recovery of their mental health and therefore contribution to the team.

SPOTTING COMMON ELEPHANTS

Why do they not change their behaviour?

No child ever gets everything they need. We all learn patterns of response that have served us well up to this point in time. That is, it has meant we have survived.* Some patterns will truly serve us well for our lives. Others can unconsciously grow an elephant between us and another person. So, always start with empathy, no matter how frustrated or annoyed you feel with someone. They are just trying to survive in a way that makes sense to them, even if it doesn't to you. They have a series of lenses you don't. Their view of the elephant is different to yours. Straight out challenge of their perspective as being 'wrong' doesn't help them or you. They need to first see you as an ally. Someone who they can trust. Who values their opinion. Who they get positive feedback from. If they feel seen by you, then they may be able to be curious about alternative perspectives on the elephant. They can then learn about the lenses they are wearing, which lead them to these default patterns of response. Default patterns of response from childhood however can be hard for people to identify, let alone see as a problem. Table 5 is designed to help you navigate common default patterns that create elephants. Use this table to help build their trust, to enable you to stop some elephants from growing in the first place.

In each of these default patterns, each person is not owning their role in growing the elephant. You can't make people change. But you have the potential to help them get curious about their ability to learn and grow. Don't dismiss them before they do.

---

* Le Pera, Dr N (2021) How to do the work: Recognise your patterns, heal from your past and create your Self. Harper Wave. USA.

Dismissing people because their view is stubbornly different is potentially missing out on a key player who has the potential to collaboratively solve the work problem you face.

Not only this. Their perspective could be the very thing that helps you shrink your own blind spots. Helping people get curious about their own lenses and supporting them in understanding a more 3D dimension of the elephant, helps you learn more about yourself.

Working with people with certain heightened characteristics can be downright draining though. I have found the work by Byron Katie[*] very useful in exploring my own response to the challenging behaviour of others. She challenges you to flip perspectives, exploring how an alternative perspective might be true. I had a particular situation where I found myself appalled

---

[*] Katie, B. with Mitchell, S. (2018). A Mind at Home with Itself: How Asking Four Questions Can Free Your Mind, Open Your Heart, and Turn Your World Around. Harper One. USA.

TABLE FIVE Navigating common workplace behaviours through connection – helping them feel seen

Presenting behaviour	**Oblivious to/denies impact of own behaviour i.e. lacks awareness.**
What might be happening for them?	These people are stuck in judging themselves by their intent, regardless of impact.
	Some people's blind spots (remember the Johari window) are bigger than others. Until they get consistent constructive feedback on their impact, they won't gain awareness. But because of the way animal brains work, they must trust you/feel seen by you, for them to get into listening mode and get curious as to what they can learn from you.
What might you do on top of the 5 Steps to Connection to build trust?	Consistently use clear, concise feedback. Use concrete, specific examples to help them shrink their blind spot.
	When this feedback comes from a place of genuine care and belief in their abilities, you will be amazed at how blind spots can shrink.

SPOTTING COMMON ELEPHANTS

Presenting behaviour	Emotional reaction, particularly to criticism/things not going to plan, that seems disproportionate to the situation.
What might be happening for them?	The person whose emotional reaction to situations seems out of kilter to the actual situation has a high level of cortisol running through their body. This is a person who, in the moment, is operating genuinely from a place of fear even though they may not be consciously aware of it.
	Various factors could be contributing to this:
	Allostatic load – this situation is the proverbial last straw that broke the camel's back.
	This is a similar situation to a prior one that didn't end well/they haven't processed and learnt from.
	Feeling out of depth/not supported.
	Deeply held patterns related to prior events, even as far back as childhood.
What might you do on top of the 5 Steps to Connection to build trust?	Take a moment each time to pause and reflect on yourself. Are they super sensitive or have you detached from your emotions in this situation? Are you making your own patterned assumption that they are ALWAYS super sensitive, and you have no part to play in how they are feeling?
	When they feel safe, then they can process things differently. This person needs a double dose of the 5 Steps to Connection.
	Make sure they feel heard in their story. Acknowledge their response, asking them to label how they feel right now, and what their perspective on the situation is. Reflect that back to them, to show them you have heard them.
	Introduce the concept of the animal brain protecting us by interpreting what we see as safe or a threat. Get them to articulate what could be just as true. Help them search for evidence of this. This helps to start training their brain to see things in a different way.
	Once you have introduced this, it becomes easier to frame up the next time (because there will be a next time), with a sentence such as:
	'I noticed when X happened, you appeared to me to be upset/angry, and it felt like a stronger emotion than I expected. I am curious as to what you are feeling and thinking right now... what might be a different perspective on this that is more helpful to you?'

Presenting behaviour	**Not taking self-responsibility. Quick to point out what others didn't do right that led to this situation. That their behaviour was the only option because of what others did.**
What might be happening for them?	This is learned helplessness. Whether from early childhood, or from significant events in life, this person has learnt a way of operating that has helped them survive. In any situation that the person picks up as threatening, the cortisol floods in and the initial reaction is to go in to freeze mode. A 'hands up in the air, it's not my fault' mode. They are worried/fearful and genuinely feel helpless. A victim of circumstance.
What might you do on top of the 5 Steps to Connection to build trust?	When something is an entrenched automatic response, it will take some time for this person to change. They operate best in a highly supportive environment where 'failing' (better described as things not turning out as hoped/expected), is seen as an opportunity to get curious and learn rather than apportion blame. So, reflect on your own behaviour as a leader. How do you respond when things go wrong? How can you consistently demonstrate curiosity and your own learning? Be vulnerable to the team in showing what you own yourself. That is, by role modelling curiosity and self-responsibility, others will start to shift too. It makes it easier to be able to then ask them to quietly reflect on what they can own/take responsibility for. Once you are consistently role modelling this self-responsibility, hold them to account for owning their behaviours too. Remember those 5Cs of self-accountability.
Presenting behaviour	**The yes person. They will do whatever you ask them to. They will consistently agree with you, and never disagree. They aim to please. Whatever you say is gospel.**
What might be happening for them?	In any situation that the person picks up as threatening, the cortisol floods in and the initial reaction is fawn mode. That is, they think that the best survival mode is to do whatever the other person asks so they can feel like they are valued. This can be inbuilt cultural deferential respect. It could be a calculated way of getting a promotion. It could be a survival technique learnt from childhood or earlier unhealthy relationships.
What might you do on top of the 5 Steps to Connection to build trust?	Now your initial reaction to this might be, what's so wrong with that? Wouldn't that make life easier? It sure would. But it wouldn't make your work better in the long run. People pleasing means one opinion dominates. For that dominating person, who is convinced they are right, it reinforces their entrenched view. It doesn't enable alternative perspectives to be explored, which is where the richness of solutions to complex problems lies. These responses can benefit from 1:1 time first, building trust through the 5 steps. Then using the approach of: 'I appreciate you want to support my/the ideas on the way forward, but what I want to hear right now is your own view. I value the experience you bring to the table. Different perspectives help us to move forward. What ideas are floating in your head?'

SPOTTING COMMON ELEPHANTS

Presenting behaviour	A strongly held belief that they are right therefore will spend time talking/demanding to be heard and/or criticising others' points of view.
What might be happening for them?	In any situation that the person picks up as threatening, the cortisol floods in and the initial reaction is to go into fight mode. This is self-preservation through and through. This person's mental model of the world genuinely has them convinced they are right. They struggle to hear other views. It feels safe to 'know'. It is important to their animal brain survival that others understand the world exactly as they see it.
What might you do on top of the 5 Steps to Connection to build trust?	Your response to a specific situation will depend on where they sit relative to you in the organisation. The same principles apply though on finding ways to elicit the oxytocin in them. When they see you as an ally, they are more likely to not undermine you, and indeed seek you out for support against others. It is when they do this that you can reinforce their value, by appreciating their perspective. Then provide a question or two that helps them to get curious on how to build their knowledge further. When the cortisol isn't running through them i.e., they don't feel under threat, they potentially have the capacity to be open to considering other perspectives.

Presenting behaviour	**Consistently talking behind people's backs.** **'Have you heard…'** **'Would you believe…'**
What might be happening for them?	Gossips come from a starting point of insecurity from low self-esteem. Passing on information about others helps people feel like they are 'in the know'. That is knowledge is power, and they have the insights others want. Gossiping can also help them feel better about themselves by judging others. Like all the other patterns, this can be ingrained from early life in the role models that person had. Judging others is a way of making people feel safe that they belong in the 'better' group but hides their insecurities. Some gossipers have an intent to harm others and see benefit in spreading a particular story. Others don't realise the impact. It is just a standard way of doing things.
What might you do on top of the 5 Steps to Connection to build trust?	Gossip is a good example of energy leakage that is better spent on solving real problems. Overall foster an environment in which people talk directly to others about their concerns. Provide as much information as you can to your teams to prevent speculation. Discourage gossip by not doing it yourself. When someone comes to talk about others, pause and then say '…and?' – which helps them articulate why they are telling you. How do you redirect their energy to the conversation they need to be having about work. Don't use secondhand information on others (gossip) to draw conclusions on people/or make decisions.

Presenting behaviour	Subtly, or not so subtly, undermining others to ensure their own self-interests are met. Criticism and blame of others, impacting culture negatively.
What might be happening for them?	Unfortunately, within your working life, depending on the size of the organisation you are working in, you are likely to come across some people whose behaviour is destructive to the culture of the organisation. Sometimes this is obvious from the beginning and sometimes they are artists at only showing certain aspects to certain people. Just like all the others above, this is an entrenched pattern of behaviour that has helped them survive in the world. In my experience, these individuals are less connected with/aware of their emotions or bottle them up and ignore them. They have learnt that power is safety and will manipulate others to get/or maintain it. Some may have cortisol spikes of fear if threatened, that have them lashing out. Others remain coldly calculating, focused on the dopamine hits of achievement/or promotion. They don't show vulnerability.
What might you do on top of the 5 Steps to Connection to build trust?	Your response to this person will depend on their relationship with you. I would still operate under the 5 steps, because a starting point of them not seeing you as a threat can be valuable. However, the ability to help them to change in my experience can be limited. I would still encourage the approach for those that think they are right, but watch carefully as toxicity is corrosive to your desired culture. If they are in your team, then tight performance management to remove them quickly is critical to the rest of the team. In the meantime, contain their impact as much as you can. Keep firm boundaries. Take good notes on interactions. Be consistent with warmth and care for the whole team including them. Keep remembering they are doing the best they can with what they have (which is searching to eliminate threat by having power over others). If they are a peer, then can you work closely with other peers to build relationships of trust so that the other person is limited in their influence? If it is your manager, or a peer who is so good at 'managing upwards', that they have their manager convinced of their brilliance, despite the toxicity others experience, I would suggest starting to look for an alternative job. Nothing is worth your health being compromised by your cortisol constantly being triggered when you work with them.

---

with a peer's behaviour. They were so adamant that they were right, that I felt my frustration rising regularly. I found myself digging my heels in and challenging their view. That didn't get me anywhere, as it had them further digging their heels in, while others around the table remained silent. Not wanting to talk

about the elephant in the room. I recognised my response, due to my own allostatic load, was not helpful. It was the ability to flip perspectives that helped me. I asked:
- What are they seeing that convinces them they are right?
- What if they are? Or at least partly?
- Does it have to be an 'either or'? Instead of trying to flip them to my perspective, could I find a combined perspective that made sense to both of us?

I reminded myself, they were doing the best they could with what they had. Assuming good intent of the best outcome for the organisation, I was able to go into future conversations consciously working to elicit oxytocin and serotonin in them. Helping them to see me as an ally. When I could calm their cortisol levels down this way, it enabled me to use one of the most powerful phrases you can have up your sleeve as a leader.

'Help me understand what you are seeing.'

One conversation doesn't make a relationship. But choosing to continually elicit those balancing chemicals and teasing out the story in their head was a great foundation to build a better relationship. It helped me understand and appreciate alternative perspectives, which increased our collaboration.

Remember the brain seeks for pattern and can discard information that doesn't support its perspective. When you find that frustration bubbling up, get curious and explore 'what if' scenarios that are different to your current view of the elephant. Consciously seeking evidence to support alternative views is helpful.

For example, when you are feeling frustrated with how someone is responding and you are thinking 'they aren't listening to me!', it is interesting to explore these alternative statements and how they might be true:

- I am not listening to them.
- They are not listening to themselves.
- I am not listening to myself.

Each of these alternative stories helps you see different options on the way forward with this person. If you are thinking 'I find them really challenging to work with', a simple alternative could be 'they find me challenging to work with'. When they aren't feeling curious yet, get curious about yourself. Change your perspective. If they could be thinking that you are difficult to work with, what might you do differently, to make it easier for them?

> *Exploring alternative perspectives helps to calm your own emotions down and opens alternative ways of seeing the opportunity in a situation.*

While your role as leader is to keep eliciting these three key chemicals for others, you also need to do that for yourself. When you are feeling your own intense emotions bubbling up in response to the behaviours of others, how can you take that deep breath. Ground yourself in connecting to who you are and the value you bring as a leader. This helps you to then curiously explore alternative perspectives. It is amazing what you can learn about yourself in the process. I know I certainly have. Just keep remembering, we are all operating from a perspective of 'truth' which is our truth because of our lenses. Start observing the patterns of response in yourself and others. Start thinking about how you will practically elicit the three key chemicals that unlock performance.

At its extreme end, the patterns of behaviour that people have learnt, start to impact their long-term health. Let's briefly explore that.

Why aren't they better by now?

'When human beings can't gain acceptance or approval from each other, they often seek attention as a replacement, even if that attention is destructive.'*

In the previous chapter I explained how a person can get caught in a vicious downward spiral because they don't feel seen or heard by others. When this continues to spiral down, it can severely impact people's mental health. This can lead them to believe the most effective method for managing this, is to submit a claim for Workers' Compensation. Given the complexities of this area, I could write a whole book on the topic. For the purposes of this book, it is worth understanding the connection between the brain science you learnt about in chapter two, the cry for help when someone chooses to put in a claim for compensation, and the way in which a person's reality impacts their recovery.

For a person to put in a claim for psychological illness in the first place, without one clearly significant traumatic incident occurring, there is some form of elephant that hasn't been addressed. Cortisol would have been flooding their body continuously, due to not being heard and understood. Be it by their manager, their peer, or even HR. Chronic cortisol grows the elephant in this person's mind. The stories that keep looping in their head, mean that every action taken by others, is seen through a lens of 'they don't understand me/care about me/listen to me'. Emotions of fear/anger/hurt do not resolve, and they become unwell.

When this person goes to their medical practitioner and is supported in putting in a claim, they feel validated. They feel heard. They get temporary relief from the cortisol, from their practitioner. If they put in their claim at work, and its validity is

---

* Clark, T.R. (2020) The 4 Stages of Psychological Safety: Defining the Path to Inclusion and Innovation. Berrett-Koehler Publishers Inc. California, USA.

challenged, it can reinforce their negative story. This deteriorates their health further. Family and health practitioners are naturally likely to side with this person, and their story, not the workplace. Further reinforcing the view of the elephant this person is experiencing. They struggle to understand why the workplace can't see it from their viewpoint only. They feel safe at home, getting oxytocin and serotonin. They feel flooded with cortisol thinking about work; therefore, they want to stay away.

The difficulty is, the longer the person stays away, disconnected, the louder the stories get, and the elephant grows even more. To be clear, if someone is completely burned out, a period focused on getting back to good sleeping, eating, drinking and exercise habits away from work, can be required, as the start to improving mental health. But if done in isolation of connection with the workplace, recovery is significantly hampered. They won't recover until they get the chronic cortisol out of their body. They can't remove cortisol effectively and return to sustainable work, when the story loop about work is a negative one.

The number and cost of psychological claims is increasing and will only get worse as this uncertain world we now live in triggers more anxiety in people. We now live in a world not only of uncertainty, but with social media algorithms that continue to reinforce holding an 'I am right' view. In this increasingly polarised world of right and wrong, it feels safe to belong to the 'right' group and direct anger elsewhere. I am not saying that leaders don't do the wrong thing, they absolutely do. But healing and getting back to green, in our mental health, is about looking inwards. It is learning about our lenses and taking full responsibility for moving forward. Not directing blame towards others. It is accepting that there are multiple angles on the elephant. But the ill person can't do this, if they don't feel you are doing the same. Create a safe environment for them to talk openly about their concerns. Where you can explore the elephant from different angles and decide how you work more effectively together.

It all starts with how you, and key others, in the workplace, can elicit oxytocin and serotonin in them. They need to feel like they belong. That they are valued as a team member. They need to feel genuinely acknowledged for the experience they have had. When they feel that, they will have greater ability to recover and return to the workplace productively. You may have some trouble accepting their view of the world, but it is their reality.

A person who is feeling anxious, or depressed, struggling to adjust to a situation in the workplace, can't hear a different perspective, until they feel heard by you.

Helping someone remove or alter a lens they are wearing, to see the elephant from a different perspective, can't happen until you first see the elephant through their lenses.

Help them feel heard, and they will heal.

It is good in these situations to start with empathy. Consider how much time you generally spend thinking about different parts of your life – work, relationships, hobbies, family, and friends etc. Then remember an injury you had or a relationship that broke down. Recall how you spent most of your time thinking about the issue. That pain can take over. Your brain keeps trying to make sense of it. When it can't, those emotions keep bubbling up. The cortisol keeps coming in. The brain is craving the balancing out of oxytocin and serotonin. If you didn't feel seen and weren't heard when you didn't have the issue, and now you are – it reinforces keeping that issue alive. This is not done consciously. It is the brain seeking belonging and only feeling that because of the illness/problem. The animal brain may want to hold on to this. To keep feeling those balancing chemicals. Create an ongoing environment that focuses on eliciting these chemicals to then enable curious learning. If an illness then occurs, recovery will be faster, because this person knows they belong in your tribe. They want to be with this important tribe in their life.

PRACTICAL STEPS:

Supporting someone with deteriorating mental health that they are blaming on the workplace

You are not expected to be an expert in psychological trauma. You do need to be an expert in caring for your team. I would encourage you to think about the following approach:

- Be disciplined in using the Five Steps to Connection, introduced at the start of the chapter.
- When someone reports feeling anxious at work or complains about others' behaviours, how can your first response to them be one of helping them feel heard. Listen to them. Validate their emotion. Acknowledge their perspective.
- Show empathy for their situation. No matter what you might think or feel about it, that is their reality. They need to feel like they are still part of your tribe.
- Get curious yourself. Don't automatically dismiss them if they are complaining about you or others. Ask yourself 'how might that be true?' Explore the alternative perspective to your automatic one about the situation. Where is communication breaking down? What behaviours might need addressing in the broader team?
- People get stuck in unhelpful stories. Help them see other explanations for how people are behaving.
- Find ways of continuing to connect so that the person's animal brain identifies you as a safe person to talk to. A person they feel seen by.

- When the person sees you as the problem, and the above isn't working yet, then find someone independent who can facilitate the conversation between the two of you, until that person can feel safe.
- See if you can get the person to agree to a three-way conversation with them and their relevant health practitioner. In this conversation, explain what you want to do in the workplace to help them recover. Demonstrate empathy and warmth in these conversations. You want the practitioner to see you as an ally in this person's recovery. Ask the medical practitioner for advice on what they see is the best way forward to help this person feel like they belong in your team and at work.

Do you see yourself?

A Board I once worked for, asked to get to know the executives in the business, beyond their day job, through a presentation. In reflecting on what to talk about, I considered the question 'What has shaped me the most into who I am today?' Our childhood does have a significant impact on us. For me, growing up the 8th of 9 children had a profound impact on me. I identified three key traits of mine that had their foundation in my childhood:
- I value community. (You had to work as a team in a large family.)
- I have a constant desire to learn. (I was born curious, then being left to my own devices as the 8th, meant I had to work out a lot for myself.)
- I am prepared to speak up where it counts. (If I didn't speak up in a large family, I wouldn't get what I wanted/needed.)

Given the reflection process was useful to me, I found myself using the question

'How has your childhood shaped how you operate today?'

with people I was coaching. Helping others reflect, helped me go deeper again, identifying a lens that I wore, that was no longer serving me. Being the 8th of 9, it was easy to get lost in the crowd. Don't get me wrong. It was a safe, warm, if somewhat hectic, family home. But I realised I didn't feel seen for whom I uniquely was as an individual. This lens, I would argue, has been incredibly useful in driving me to achieve a range of positive things that did get me noticed. That led me to a range of promotions and amazing opportunities. I could recognise though, as I got older, that I was still wearing the lens of 'you don't see me'. This leant me to experiencing unhelpfully strong negative emotions, when I wasn't understood and appreciated by people 'in power'. (I do put this in parenthesis, as you choose who has power over how you feel.) It made me feel like I was different and didn't belong. It was an unhelpful lens that had got too sensitive. By choosing to get curious and flip perspectives, I had an uncomfortable 'ah ha' moment. I realised that the issue wasn't whether others saw me or not, as I have no control of this. The issue was I didn't see myself. Recognising that story when it comes up (because long held stories can take a little while to fully disappear), enables me to flip the story to 'I see myself', eliciting that feeling of grounded strength. From there I can get curious about both what I am doing, and the other person's lenses.

    Let's face it, you will never have everyone approve of you the way you would like. They all wear their own lenses. You can't control what others think of you. What matters is you truly seeing and embracing yourself. Through this you can learn a better way to navigate the world. Through this, you will identify elephants earlier and minimise their growth. Never underestimate how much value you will unlock by learning more about yourself.

In committing to lifelong learning about myself, I use a journal. Writing down my thoughts and feelings, and examining them, has helped me continue to learn about myself and my lenses. I am a better leader and human being because of it.

I am fascinated by what feels like the endless layers that I discover about myself as I grow older. Just as I think I really understand myself I find another lens.

Curiosity about yourself, helps you shrink elephants.

When you find yourself amid conflict, or stepping in to help others, remember it could be you that has also contributed to the elephant. Remember you have blind spots. Committing to lifelong learning helps you shrink your own blind spots that contribute to elephants.

PRACTICAL STEPS:

How well do you know yourself?

I encourage you to become a journal writer if you haven't already. Use these reflection questions to help kick off your learning journey about the lenses that influence your view of the elephant.

- What lenses are you consciously aware of?
- 60–80% of our thoughts are negative and the brain will therefore go astray if left unchecked.[*] This is the animal brain seeking threat. These thoughts influence your actions unconsciously. You need to bring your conscious awareness to these thoughts. Seek the more helpful stories that help you focus productively.

---

[*] Gawdat, M. with Law, A. (2024) Unstressable: A Practical Guide to Stress-free Living. Bluebird. Pan McMillan. Hampshire. England.

- What thoughts and emotions keep bubbling up for you? Tap into these. They give an insight into how your animal brain is perceiving the world. Learning to see the signs that cortisol is triggered will help you manage it.
- Your pre-existing thoughts and feelings about any person are a lens that biases your automatic actions. Become consciously aware of how you perceive someone. Don't let preconceived views amplify conflict.
- What's your own allostatic load at the time of any conflict you face? How much could shift by you choosing to do activities that elicit oxytocin and serotonin for you, before heading into difficult conversations with others?
- All you have is your own perspective, through your own lenses. You have one view of the elephant. Others have legitimate views too. How curious are you really?

Take some time here to reflect and journal on what has happened in your life:

- What patterns of behaviours can you identify in you from early childhood?
- What might parents/siblings/friends recall of your typical behaviours as a child, particularly when things weren't easy?
- What then have been the most significant events in your life?
- How have they shaped your view of the world? Of yourself?
- What lenses might your experiences have added?

The nuance of a conversation with a peer/manager

Elephant shrinking conversations with peers and managers are far more likely to be rationalised into non-existence, than with

direct reports. There is an increased discomfort, given the very different power dynamic, yet this is one of the biggest blockers to organisational effectiveness. There are some nuances however to peer and manager conversations, that are worth considering.

When you find that emotion bubbling up, it can be more intense with a peer or manager, than a direct report, as it can feel much harder to influence or 'control' them. Particularly if you have competing objectives or are relying closely on them to achieve your result. When you feel frustrated with them, it can be natural to want to criticise them. Be it openly, or behind their back. This 'itch' not disappearing within a short few hours, is a good indicator that you need to have a conversation with them. But consider what they might be frustrated with you about. What reflection can you do on yourself first? So you come into a conversation with acknowledgement of how you could approach things differently too.

FIGURE TEN

The 5 components of understanding an elephant from two perspectives

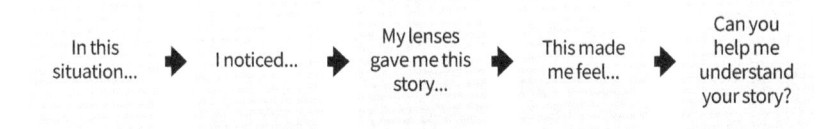

In this situation... ➡ I noticed... ➡ My lenses gave me this story... ➡ This made me feel... ➡ Can you help me understand your story?

When you want to understand an emerging elephant with a peer or manager, experiment with 5 components* to frame up the conversation. Let's step through the five components of this conversation (Figure 10).

---

* Combining the work of the Centre for Creative Leadership on the SBI model (ccl.org), with our elephant lenses, and a dose of curiosity.

'In this situation': The specific time and place – not an 'always or you never'. For example, 'I want to talk to you about earlier today/last week when we were...'

'I noticed': The objective behaviour that anyone observing would be able to see. It has no judgement attached to it. For example, 'you didn't arrive on time', 'you spoke over me', 'you rolled your eyes when I said...'

'My lenses gave me this story': Recognise that your perspective is how you are making sense of the situation, which is likely different to theirs.

This made me feel: This is you owning the emotion that has emerged because of the story you have in your head about that person's actions. What exactly are you feeling? Frustrated? Annoyed? Perplexed? Hurt? Angry? Worried? Uncertain? Upset? Be honest with yourself and them.

'Can you help me understand your story': You have chosen to be vulnerable in owning your own story. Now it is time to step back and listen to theirs. This gives you a clearer joint understanding of the elephant. Joint appreciation of the different angles shrinks the elephant to a manageable size for both of you.

Here is an example of a conversation I had with a manager using this framework:

'I looked at your comments on my Board paper and noticed you had suggested that I reconsider the way I wrote X. My lenses gave me this story that you wanted me to hide certain information from the Board. That story made me feel uncomfortable. Can you help me understand the intent behind your comments?'

Can you see how this can enable a less defensive response from this manager? This is me acknowledging that it was my own story, through my lenses, that had me feeling uncomfortable. I am also assuming their good intent. I just want to understand it. They were able to clearly explain they didn't want to hide information. Rather, they had an alternative perspective on the situation. By raising and discussing our views, we shrank the elephant. If I hadn't raised it, I know this would have created doubts in my mind about them. These doubts would have grown the elephant. The conversation was early on in our relationship. This conversation played an incredibly important part in strengthening the trust between us. We worked even closer together, because of our trust in our ability to shrink emerging elephants together.

Both at peer and manager level, just choosing this honest conversation, is sometimes all you need. If you can't resolve your differences with a peer, it is reasonable to say

'This feels like a tough one for us to find common ground on. Why don't we get our manager/another peer, we both trust, to help us get aligned'.

I will cover more on if they refuse this, in Chapter 6.

If a peer or manager criticises you, it is valuable to take a few deep breaths before responding. This enables you to stop and take in what they are saying. Even if it isn't constructive or given without the full context of the situation. Your first step is to control your initial burst of cortisol. Before you say something, you will later regret. That can be hard when you feel they have a blind spot on their own behaviour and won't own it. It is easy to get defensive.

One of the hardest lessons I have had to learn, is recognising that some people in senior roles remain at a level of awareness of self that they have put armour around. Believing they are right. Not interested in learning more about themselves. Or truly listening to others. It is not your role to push them to take responsibility for what they need to own. Your role is to keep learning about yourself, while gaining insights into them. You can only change yourself. Others must choose to change themselves. And if they don't, then accept the consequences of their impact. Helping them get curious absolutely helps. But it starts with you being curious about yourself.

When you find feedback unhelpful, try questions such as:
- *'Can you help me understand the context more?'* or
- *'Can you tell me more?'* or
- *'That's hard to hear given my intent. I'd like to reflect on this'* (Buy yourself time to balance out that cortisol for yourself. You can come back to the next conversation with a calmer mind.)

When addressed early, sometimes it only takes one conversation, to recognise the different lenses you are wearing and see the elephant easily, from both perspectives. Particularly if you have been used to using this common language. Other times it will take longer but do persevere. When you find yourself rationalising not talking, take a deep breath. Don't let fear rule your career. See it as an amazing opportunity to become a more impactful leader.

Your lenses will always create blind spots. They wax and wane, depending on the combination of people you are working with at any point in time, and the lenses they wear. Become aware of your emotional response to situations. Learn to take that deep breath. Get curious about your contribution to the elephant. The faster you can do this, the faster the elephant shrinks to a workable size. To be an impactful leader, you need to keep doing this inner work.

PRACTICAL STEPS:

How you can learn more about the lenses you wear.

Go back to Table 5 earlier in the chapter. Can you see yourself in any of these? How can you consciously elicit your own oxytocin and serotonin, to enable yourself to get into a calmer space? Allowing you to get curious about what drives your own perspective. Ask yourself 'what's an alternative perspective? What evidence can I gather that supports this perspective?'

Be consciously aware that you have biases. As soon as you remind yourself of this, you can help get yourself curious about different perspectives. You won't ever get rid of all your biases. But you can become more aware of them.

A good place to start in your journey is to stop and reflect on your responses to conflict in the past. Choose a couple of, ideally recent examples, where you have been aware of conflict in your workplace. Write in your journal on the following questions:

- What was the situation as you saw it?
- What emotion/s do you recall feeling at the time?
- What was the story you had in your head on what was driving other people's behaviour?
- What was the story in your head that had you decide to respond in the way you did? It is interesting to see here if you can identify the story that was there in the moment versus the story that perhaps bubbles up later as your rationale for your actions. This is a standard human response. Remember our brains want to keep us safe, so the story we have in our head is part of feeling ok about ourselves and our actions.
- What might this situation tell you about your strengths and the lenses your wear?

The more you journal on your response to conflict, the more you can examine those lenses. Reflection enables you to learn about yourself.

- The next step is to apply this learning by trying a different approach next time. This is you evolving into a conflict-confident elephant shrinker.
- Journal to prepare for challenging conversations with the Five Components of understanding an elephant. This helps you get into the focused space needed. Reflect afterwards on how you went. What can you learn about yourself from this conversation? What patterns showed up for you in your emotions? What is the story in your head? Is it useful or not? What's a more useful story to tell yourself?
- What are your current assumptions about the people you work with? Of those, which ones are negative/not helpful? If you assume people are doing the best they can with what they have got, what's an alternative perspective you could take?
- Whilst specific feedback in the moment is far more helpful for in the moment learning, welcome periodic 360-degree feedback. (Where you get anonymous feedback from your manager, your peers, and your team.) Can I say I have never loved 360-degree feedback. I don't know many people who do. I find my cortisol goes into overdrive. Without the context of the situation, it is hard to make sense of what people are saying. The gold though, is in repeat 360s over time that can show if a consistent pattern presents for you. That is different people giving you similar feedback, indicating a persistent lens (for better or worse). A great question to ask yourself before you reject the feedback is 'how might that be true?'
- Remember you have a particular view of the elephant in your brain. Others will see the elephant differently. When a particular negative story keeps popping into your head, get curious about it. Write it down. What is the threat that your animal brain is picking up? What might an alternative, more useful story be?

SPOTTING COMMON ELEPHANTS

Key things to remember

In this chapter you have explored some of the common behaviours that can show up in the workplace and grow elephants if not addressed. You have learnt some strategies to work with them, including **The Five Steps to connection:**
1. **Find common ground** with them that has nothing to do with work and bring that into conversation regularly.
2. Observe to find out where their strengths lie and help them **play to strengths.**
3. Reflect on how you **intentionally recognise strengths** and thank them for it.
4. Help them get curious by **asking curious questions.**
5. **Acknowledge changed behaviour** and check in with them to see how they are.

You have then looked at how ill health and Workers' Compensation provide an additional layer of complexity – where this story is so loud for the person, they struggle to hear anything else. But you can avoid this scenario, by consciously helping that person to feel heard.

You have learnt some useful questions to ask yourself when tension starts to build from having different perspectives:
- How might that be true?
- What might be a different explanation? What evidence could support that?

You have learnt the **Five components of understanding an elephant from two perspectives**
- In this situation...
- I noticed...
- My lenses gave me this story...

- This made me feel...
- Can you help me understand your story?

Now that you can observe and start to recognise common patterns of behaviours in yourself and others, let's dive into the next section on applying these skills in the context of unresolving/escalating conflict.

SECTION TWO: CAN YOU HALT ITS GROWTH?

CHAPTER FOUR

THE SUPPORT YOU NEED TO SHRINK ELEPHANTS

You have spent the first part of the book thinking about the reality of our different perspectives of an elephant, that contributes to inevitable conflict when not talked about. You also have some simple tools you can now use to **minimise conflict through great connection, contribution and curiosity**. While these strategies do work, they won't work always. The lenses people wear complicate matters. This next section of the book explores how to shrink what I call persistent smaller, but growing, elephants. Those elephants that have grown just big enough to shift conflict from being quiet, to a little bit noisy. You may be directly involved and feeling the heat of tension yourself. It may be your team coming to you for help with conflict they are dealing with. Either way, this is an opportunity for you to choose to use your elephant shrinking skills. This chapter helps you gather key resources, before you start a conversation with others about a persistent elephant.

We are tribal creatures.

Conflict can be seen as a threat to the tribe.

We would prefer to not experience this discomfort. When you have a rush of cortisol from this discomfort, your perspective gets distorted. All your past experiences, with this or similar situations, are processed ridiculously quickly by your animal brain. Maybe you do have a reasonable perspective on the situation. It doesn't mean however, that there aren't alternative perspectives, that are valuable to consider. Your ability to disconnect from this initial 'threat' and consider alternative ways of seeing the elephant is key.

Just like you need to play a role in helping elicit the three counterbalancing chemicals in other's brains, you also need to do that for yourself continuously, when faced with conflict.

Learning to recognise your own cortisol spikes, having a framework of questions to use, and having your own sounding board of people to guide you, will help you navigate the discomfort in the tribe.

Given a tendency by some to off load conflict to the HR department[*] to deal with as soon as it bubbles up, in this chapter I will:
- Explore your role as a leader versus the HR department.
- Provide you with a checklist of questions to consider those ecosystem layers of elephants we talked about in chapter one (system, team and individual).

---

[*] This department is often called 'People and Culture' or similar names. I am choosing HR as a globally recognised term.

- Set out valuable support people to have around you, to help you keep perspective and not feel alone in these times.

I have asked HR to lean in

Conflict can lead to frustrations when you just want to get the job done and this elephant is slowing it down. When leaders are in this space of conflict, a common reaction is to call HR. To get them to help resolve the matter. While there is nothing wrong with seeking support of people who, hopefully, are experts in effectively managing conflict, it is important that you stop for a moment and consider your role versus that of HR.

> *Despite the title often used of 'People and Culture', it is not HR's primary role to create a healthy culture in your teams/ organisation. Because they can't. Only you as the leader of your team can create the culture of that team.*

You are leading and therefore influencing that team (for better or worse) day in and day out. HR can provide guidance on processes to follow. They can provide training on leadership. They can provide legal support. They may even be able to coach you, or at least find a coach for you. But you need to be clear. The base role of HR in this situation, is risk management, to protect the company. Your base role in leadership is to create the right culture for your teams, to bring out their full potential.

If you can't demonstrate that you can effectively resolve conflict and rather abdicate to HR to solve, it ultimately weakens your position as a leader.

THE SUPPORT YOU NEED TO SHRINK ELEPHANTS

You need to demonstrate consistently how you constructively face the discomfort of persistent elephants, so your team learns to do the same.

Otherwise, when inevitable conflict arises for them, they will do what you do. You may then find yourself frustrated, when they don't build effective relationships. When they don't address minor conflict, that is getting in the way of getting the job done. But if you haven't set the example, what else can you expect? You may be lucky to have an HR business partner who has operations and conflict management experience. This is incredibly valuable. They can be an excellent sounding board. But they don't have the full context. They don't know your people like you do.

HR follow the formula; you have the nuance. You own your teams. You own the culture in your teams. You need to set the example.

Think about conflict as a car starting to speed up. You never want to assume someone else is driving this. It is your team, your people, your issue to resolve. Yes, there is discomfort. People's behaviour can baffle you. I may have been shrinking elephants for years, learning more every time about people's lenses, (including my own), but I don't relish conflict and the intense emotions around it. It does however get easier with practice. Shrinking elephants early, keeps you in the driver's seat and slows the car down, to a manageable speed for everyone in it.

To be clear, when there are potential legal implications, HR has a clear role to play. I'll cover the decisions and process of that in Chapter 7. This middle section of the book though, is all about shrinking an elephant before it grows to a point of causing very loud, difficult conflict.

Through this process remember:
- **You own the culture**, therefore the pervasive behaviours in your team. You are the conductor of this choir – observing, encouraging, acknowledging, coaching, role modelling.
- **You are responsible for finding ways to consistently trigger the three balancing chemicals** of oxytocin, serotonin, and dopamine in your team. Offsetting the cortisol, which will always pop up.
- **You are responsible for enabling creative conflict** to debate complex problems and their solutions, **while reducing social conflict** in your team. This is about appreciating multiple perspectives. People respectfully working to ensure people feel heard.
- HR generalists provide forms they want issues recorded on. They will want to ensure the right process is followed. They may provide a training module on the process. If you trust them, they may be part of your sounding Board. They may help coach you through (I'll talk about that further below).
- HR legal team/investigators answer the questions: 'Is it bullying and/or harassment? Is it a breach of the code of conduct? Have they broken the law? What are the legal employment consequences?' (See Chapter 7 for when you pull them in.)
- A Workers' Compensation insurer decides if the workplace has been a significant contributing factor to a psychological illness claim. Whether 'reasonable management action' has taken place. (Note: this is fraught with challenges. Your focus on shrinking elephants is to minimise the likelihood of people getting to a point that they submit a claim).

> *You are responsible for maintaining the personal relationships and the long-term play of the team.*

You are the leader of this team. Others have their vested interest and roles, and you have yours. Think how you would feel if you had tension with your manager or colleague and your manager hand balled it to someone else to 'deal with'. The first thing you know is someone in HR is saying 'I heard there was some conflict you were involved in that I need to talk to you about'. That doesn't feel like a vote of confidence in you, does it? So don't do it to your team. Your role as a leader is to always be willing to step into the discomfort of conflict and shrink the elephant.

The rest of this chapter will give you some simple tools to help you feel ready, even if your heart is racing.

―――

The power of a great question

When I have played a key leadership role in emergency response, each nominated person has a checklist, as a guide. Even though I felt experienced enough to know what I was doing, I would always do a check against this framework of questions. It's a simple but powerful way, to keep your brain focused, through a critical time.

When you decide to step in to learn about the elephant, you don't want to go in blind.

There is power in your intentionality.

This isn't about spending ages to prepare. As you will learn later, response times are critical when things start to boil over. You will, however, have greater positive impact, when you are fully present and planned. Some short, sharp focusing questions, will help you get grounded in caring curiosity.

Confucius says:

'The one who knows all the answers has not been asked all the questions'

When someone believes they are right, and have all the answers, this is their animal brain working to protect them. Holding to a pattern of interpretation that makes sense to them. It is hard to get curious when feeling threatened. Preparing before a conversation, gets you curious. It helps you frame a conversation that can get the other person curious.

The framework of questions in the following Practical Steps, helps you to be in the right frame of mind to explore the layers of the ecosystem. To then identify potential elephants. I would encourage you to use a journal, to start answering those questions. If you are honest and aware, that your own emotions in relation to the situation are intense, you may want someone to help you work through the questions. These questions are relevant, whether you are involved directly with conflict or are choosing to step in to coach one of your team through the process.

Remember, to every situation, you will bring your lenses that influence your perspective. You then add additional lenses, unique to this situation (see Figure 11). What stories might be going through your head, that influence your perspective on this situation?

Heading into a conversation around conflict, you need to understand the impact you have on others. You don't ever intend to make things worse. But how you show up, with those lenses you have on, unconsciously influences how you behave, therefore how you are perceived by others.

'We judge others by their behaviour and ourselves by our intent'*

---

* Covey, S. (2020). The Seven Habits of Highly Effective People. Simon & Schuster, Australia. USA.

PRACTICAL STEPS:

Preparing to have a conversation about a persistent elephant

Where am I?

- What are the emotions and stories in my head right now about this situation?
- What is my own allostatic load?
- Can I be curious here?

What do I currently know about the Individual/s involved?

- What do I know about them and their background?
- What do I know about what has happened to them recently?
- What do I have in common with them that creates a sense of safe connection with them?
- What are their strengths?

Team

- What evidence of impact on the team is there at this point?
- Who might I need to speak to beyond the individual to understand further context?

System

- What's happening at work right now that contributes to the pressure cooker?
- What am I aware of that is causing frustration?

Self-reflection

- What expectations have I placed on this individual/s?
- How fully present and listening have I been in recent interactions?
- Thinking about this, how might I be contributing to this tension?

FIGURE ELEVEN

What are your own stories about this conflict?

- I don't have time for this
- I am finding home life hard
- I don't feel secure about my job
- The team just want it to go away
- I have so much to do right now
- This person is interfering with my goals
- This person lacks insight

The secret sauce in shrinking the elephant, is to start with questions on yourself. This doesn't mean rationalising not talking to others until 'you work yourself out'. Rather this is acknowledging that you wear lenses. Your lenses influence your perspective. Strong emotions bubbling up indicate a lens or two at play. That has you seeing the elephant, from a very different perspective to the other person or people. Tuning into what is going on in your head first, is valuable.

PRACTICAL STEPS:

Recognising your own lenses before having a conversation

Sometimes the first step in not putting your head in the sand, is to have the uncomfortable conversation with yourself. If you are the one feeling the annoyance/frustration/anger at others who seem oblivious, it is useful to ask yourself the following questions:

- What is the emotion I am feeling? Where is it showing up in my body? What story have I got stuck in my head about what the other person is doing that is causing this emotion? Can I literally shake this off through star jumps/a walk around the block?
- What might be an alternative perspective on what that other person is doing that isn't about deliberately antagonising me?
- What are my own self-doubts/insecurities that are my own issues to deal with? What might this tell me about what there is to learn about myself in this situation?
- Before you have the conversation ask yourself:
  - Am I ready?
  - Am I focused, able to fully listen and stay curious?
  - Have I got my own challenges I need to process first?

When you recognise you may have contributed to the situation, it is useful to open the conversation with this vulnerability. This helps build further connection with the other person. You could kick off a conversation with:

> **'I recognise there are things I am working on here and I may have contributed to the issues. Could we work on this together to get to a common understanding of the elephant and what our joint actions will be to shrink it?'**

Curiosity from everyone is at the heart of shrinking elephants.

When you remain curious about the situation, you may find something you can practically change in your behaviour, the team or the environment, which shrinks the elephant quickly. At the very least, you come with empathy into the conversations you are about to have.

As time goes on you will get more and more confident in sensing the elephants early. You will gently step in, with an understanding of all the ecosystem layers, to work with others to shrink the elephant to a manageable size. When you first own your role as a leader who shrinks elephants though, it can be uncomfortable. You can benefit from targeted support.

Who is on your Board?

Having a Board isn't saying you aren't up to managing conflict. Having a Board says you are wise. You recognise that your own lenses will give a view of the elephant. You need people with different lenses to help shift that view as needed. While I have had years of elephant shrinking and teach people how to approach it, if I am stepping into intense conflict, I will always make sure I have the right support around me. My Board helps me to navigate moving around the elephant, to get a 3D perspective faster.

I want a Board I can trust, who can get me curious on the questions:
- Where have I lost perspective here?
- What's a different way of viewing this?
- What are my options here?
- What am I not seeing?

FIGURE TWELVE

You are the CEO of your life. Who is on your Board?

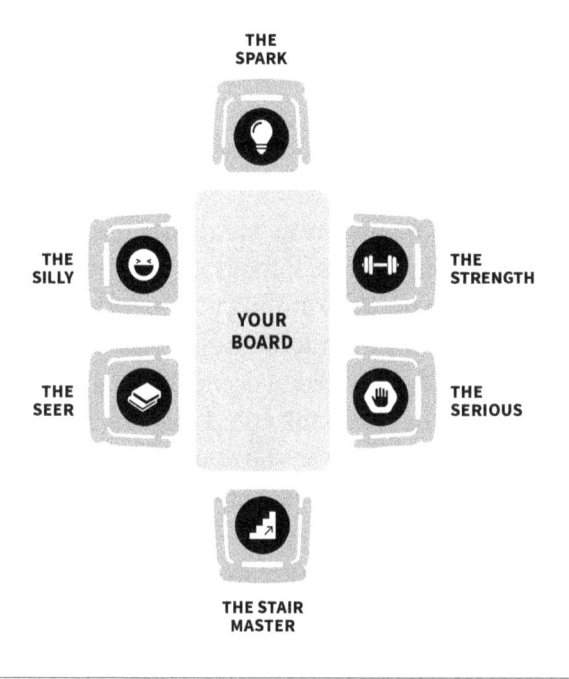

```
                    THE
                    SPARK
                     💡

    THE                              THE
    SILLY  😀         YOUR    🏋    STRENGTH
                      BOARD
    THE                              THE
    SEER   📖                 ✋    SERIOUS

                    THE STAIR
                    MASTER
```

Regardless of your actual title in the workplace, it is useful to think of yourself as the CEO of the teams you lead. The most successful CEOs have a good Board. They turn to them for advice, on the variety of subjects they are juggling. Don't do it alone. You will need a different Board though, depending on the issues you are facing. You need specific voices around your Board table for shrinking elephants.* (Figure 12)

---

* Adapted for conflict from 'Who is on your Board' from Hawkins, G. (2020). Mentally at Work: Optimising health and business performance through connection. Mentally at Work. Melbourne, Australia.

As you read through each of these roles, write down, in that journal you have, who might play them, for you. The principles are:
- No one person can effectively play all roles, although they may play a couple.
- You may want more than one person for one role.
- It is good to have a combination of people inside and outside your workplace to give different perspectives.

Here are the roles you need:
- **Spark:** Who gives you inspiration and energy around the benefits you get from shrinking elephants with others? Who inspires you to want to step in? Who among your peers has this as their genius power? I know, in facilitating workshops, I often talk about authors being my spark. For me this is Brené Brown and Esther Perel. Maybe this book could play the role of sparking your belief in, energy for and the courage to step in.
- **Strength:** Who helps you access your confidence when you feel a bit shaky? When you doubt your skills? I recommend having a couple of people for this role. One inside and one outside of your workplace. Ideally, one of them is your manager. When you are facing into discomfort, it is good to not only keep your manager informed but feel they have your back. You need to make the judgement call though, if they have enough insight. If they don't or contribute to the current issue, they can't play this role effectively.
- **Serious:** Who is the person who cares enough to point out the potential pitfalls along the way? That is, help you to manage the risk. An HR manager can play a key role here, as can someone who is experienced in stepping into these situations outside the organisation.
- **Stair master:** Who can help hold you to account for each step along the way? This may be an HR account manager, or your own manager.

- **Seer:** Who has had lots of experience in this space and knows you well? This isn't about HR experience in process. This is about both deep experience with people and someone who sees the potential in you as a leader. Shrinking elephants is an opportunity for your growth as a leader. For you to build the capability of your team, to do the same. You will benefit though from wise advice along the way, that encourages you not just to face the elephant in the room, but also step into your growth potential. Every adversity is an opportunity for growth. You need someone who believes in your future impact as a leader, to help unlock your learning. This could be an executive coach.
- **Silly:** Let's face it. These experiences can sap you of energy. They can be painful. Laughter is an incredible perspective taker. It robs pain of its power. It renews your energy. So, make sure you have some funny friends.

It is not unusual, when someone reflects on this exercise, that they can't find everyone they need straight away. When this is the case, I would encourage you to ask your peers and HR for introductions.

Key things to remember

You can't do it alone. Accept everyone needs help.

Find that help. Everything will become easier with help.

In preparing to shrink an elephant you will now understand:
- **You, not HR, are responsible for the dynamics of the people in your team.** For creating connection in the first place and helping everyone understand and shrink elephants. Before they become a significant problem.
- HR have a role in guiding when a formal process is needed. Legal resources provide technical advice. While it is important to respect the process, you should **never let an HR process derail you from your role as a leader.** Continually find ways to elicit oxytocin and serotonin in all of those involved in conflict, to shrink the elephant faster. If the process doesn't make sense, seek to understand and change it with HR. Don't be a passenger.
- **Questions help you get curious.** They are an effective way of making sure you are in the best frame of mind to have the conversations.
- **When you find your own emotions bubbling up, get curious** about the insight it gives you into your own lenses. What story is looping in your head? There is an opportunity for your own growth here.
- **Assemble your elephant shrinking board around you,** to help you stay curious to the different perspectives of the elephant.

Once you have reflected on those questions and have your Board assembled, it is time to start shrinking elephants. Chapter 5 will walk you through the principles for doing this.

CHAPTER FIVE

THE FIVE PRINCIPLES OF SHRINKING AN ELEPHANT

If you don't talk it out, you'll act it out. *

Having led or reviewed many investigations into complex safety events and psychological claims, I have learnt to stick with five principles, where conflict is evident (see Figure 13). These principles hold true, regardless of whether the actual situation involves you directly or you are coaching someone who is having the conversation.

1. <u>Safety first always:</u> Remember when the brain perceives threat, cortisol drives an automatic response. ALL parties need to feel safe, throughout the process, to actively engage.

---

* Grenny, J., Paterson, K., McMillan, R., Switzler, A., Gregory, E. (2021) Crucial Conversations (3rd edition). Tools for Talking When Stakes are High. McGraw Hill. New York, USA.

FIGURE THIRTEEN

The 5 principles of shrinking elephants

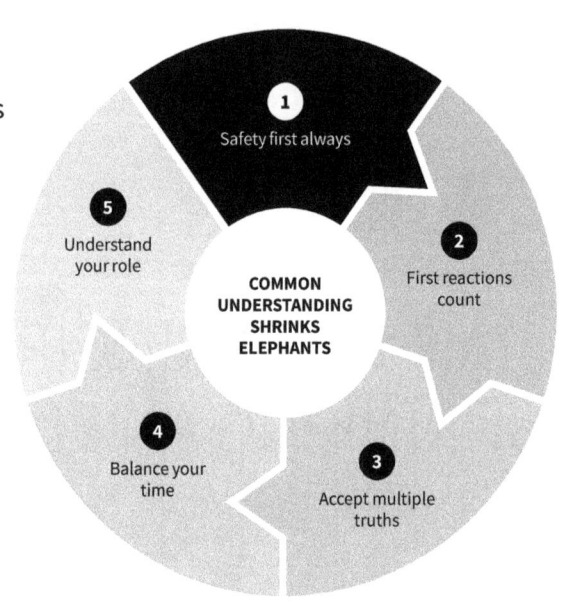

Diagram: A circular wheel labeled "COMMON UNDERSTANDING SHRINKS ELEPHANTS" in the center, divided into 5 segments:
1. *Safety first always*
2. *First reactions count*
3. *Accept multiple truths*
4. *Balance your time*
5. *Understand your role*

2. <u>Initial reactions count:</u> Whether someone comes to you, or you initiate the conversation, your initial reaction to them will significantly influence the outcome. You need to remain open, caring and curious.
3. <u>Accept multiple truths:</u> Remain curious to the situation and to yourself – There is no one truth in conflict – just a variety of perspectives. Everyone is biased including you! Recognise your own responses and explore alternative truths.
4. <u>Balance your time:</u> Don't speed through the conversations as people won't feel heard. Don't take too long to decide upon action, as people won't feel heard.
5. <u>Understand your role:</u> Don't solve it for them. Your role is to build the curiosity muscle in all parties, (including you), in a safe environment. This helps unearth the unhelpful stories.

It is only through unearthing everyone's stories – both conscious and unconscious, that those involved can begin to work out a way forward. You 'rescuing' others, or pushing to move on quickly, doesn't shrink the elephant.

Let's unpack these a bit more.

―――――

Principle One: Safety first always

When an elephant has grown to a point, that even if you wanted to ignore it, it would be hard to, people's brains will be in a heightened state of threat. Significant cortisol will be flooding through them. Consciously, or unconsciously, they will be assessing whether they go back in a shell, fall apart or attack. (Which, in conflict, often comes out as pointing out what the other party is doing wrong, and how badly they have been treated). In their mind, consciously or unconsciously, they are asking

'Are you a friend or a foe?'

Their body is tense. Disagreeing with them at this point, increases their cortisol. You become an additional threat! Until the person/people directly involved in the conflict can genuinely feel safe with you, they will struggle to listen, let alone accept other perspectives. Their brain will be unconsciously asking:

'Do you see me? Do you hear me? Do you value me?'

Be forgiving of their reactions. You may think their view is irrational or ill thought through, but they are doing the best they can with what they have. Their reactions give you great insights into their story and some of the lenses they wear. Observe and reflect on this. But do not go into rational process mode with cortisol.

Cortisol needs care. Conflict needs care.

All that you have learned to date, on the importance of the balancing chemicals, comes into play when you step into these conversations. Your first role is helping the person to feel safe in your presence. They need to feel like you understand them. That, regardless of this conflict, you value them. Through the whole process of resolving the issues, they need to keep feeling this. This isn't a once and we're done action. This person will continually need to experience oxytocin and serotonin, to help their brain get back to a calmer state. To be able to be curious about other perspectives. Whether the person is in your team, or a peer, when you are stepping into shrinking elephants, you need to be constantly aware that cortisol will keep spiking. Balance this out, with oxytocin and serotonin, to help them then get curious, to get dopamine firing.

If you have serious concerns about the person's mental state, it is important to seek further help. This is about listening and asking gentle questions. Find out who else they have in their personal life. Connect with them right away, to help the person get the professional help they need. If you have an employee assistance program, you may want to stay with the person, while you connect them to someone there, or a relevant public support program.[*]

Conflict is not pleasant for anyone. It is natural to feel alone.

---

[*] In Australia call Lifeline on 13 11 14, or Beyond Blue on 1300 224 636

Keep tuning in to how they are behaving and intentionally create a safe environment again and again. 'Safety comes first' is not just because it is important to value other people. Safety is needed to resolve conflict.

> *'A judgement/critical comment, or even general great piece of advice, will not be accepted before one feels fundamentally understood, liked and accepted."*

The principle 'safety first always' also applies to you. You need to ask yourself…'Do you feel safe?' If you are taking the lead here and the other person isn't initially open, this can trigger your own cortisol spikes. That may not be helpful. 'Safety first always' means getting your Board lined up before you step in. Keep checking in with them, particularly the 'Strength', along the way. Create your own safe environment to give you the courage to stay curious.

Principle Two – First reactions count

You have an animal brain, just like everyone else. When someone chooses to be vulnerable with you, about the conflict they are experiencing, please remember it will trigger unconscious protective responses in you. You may have a heap of other work on and feel like you don't have time for this. You may have your own conflicts you are dealing with. You may not have slept well last night. You may already have pre-conceived views of this person. Alternatively, you may be choosing to vulnerable with a

---

* The Gottman Institute at www.gottman.com

peer or manager and they have a cortisol spike and don't respond well. Regardless of the specifics, when you are faced with other people's emotions, you need to stay in a calm, curious state, to get the best outcome.

Staying calm and curious is much easier, if you have a strong connection with them already. Hence why I chose to spend time up front getting you familiar with the Five Steps to Connection. If you don't have that connection, the other person will feel that too. An eyebrow raised, a distracted response or a non-emotional response from you, could be seen as a threat. Is that completely logical to your conscious brain? Likely no. Nor to most people observing from a distance. However, you need to accept the animal brain will work in weird and wonderful ways. When cortisol is firing, lack of connection, indeed lack of anything but a caring response, will be picked up as a threat.

Think of your own experiences of cortisol spikes, at a simple level. Your plane has been cancelled, meaning you are going to miss a critical meeting. Your animal brain releases a cortisol surge. It demands an immediate reaction. You then approach staff at the gate desk. You find them to be rather short and matter of fact on what they can do for you, which isn't much. You find yourself with a surge of annoyance, which leaves you saying things that are less than productive. You can cause conflict when you don't even know the person, because of your own cortisol levels. Imagine how much more impact an uncontrolled cortisol response has, when you know each other and had assumed there would be support.

Many a Workers' Compensation psychological claim has had a common theme of lack of support. 'It wasn't the event itself, but how I felt treated by my manager when I told them, that I can't get over'. This is a person who feels under threat. When they don't get that immediate care, they see a pattern of 'you too are against me'. Leading to withdrawing from work and work relationships.

Seeking people outside work, to prop up their view of the world as the only right one. First reactions have a profound ripple effect, so, make them count.

You are human and sometimes your response isn't ideal. Good leaders will have a discipline of self-reflection, at the end of each day, to stop and consider how they show up. When you recognise you haven't shown up at your best, when someone reached out to you for support, (be it team member, peer or manager), then seek them out as soon as possible face to face. (Or if not in the same location, via video conference) and try something like:

> *'I apologise for my behaviour yesterday when you raised x situation. That may have left you not feeling so great about me and my support of you. I genuinely value who you are and how you contribute. It was other issues that I am juggling, that had me responding in what was perhaps a less then helpful way. I am sorry for the impact it may have had on you. Can we talk now about, or set aside a time to talk about, what you are experiencing? I want to better understand how to help.'*

I have dealt with complaints, where the manager hasn't reacted well, and then dug in their heels, defending their response. Which has, in some cases, led to a Workers' Compensation claim. Likewise, I have seen the power of a vulnerable manager. A manager prepared to acknowledge, directly to the person, that they could have done better. Damage can be reversed, if this acknowledgement is swift. First reactions count. Your next move counts even more, when that first reaction wasn't ideal.

It doesn't matter if you see them as a future talent of the team or someone who perhaps needs to find a role that is better suited to them. When they are experiencing threat, they need to know they belong at that point in time. If they see you as someone who

PRACTICAL STEPS:

Being prepared so your initial reaction to conflict is one of support

Given how critical those first reactions are, think about doing the following:

- Use the Five Steps to connection to build a foundation of strong relationships with your team. (Find common ground, Play to strengths; Intentionally recognise strengths; Ask curious questions; and Acknowledge changed behaviour.)
- Learn to take that deep breath on a regular basis in any situation. Become aware of when you feel emotions rise in you. Take one slow conscious breath before intentionally deciding what the most effective response (rather than reaction) is.
- If you are choosing to have a conversation before someone raises the issue with you, go back to your questions from Chapter 4 for help. Are you ready? Are you fully present?
- When you are in the middle of other work, and someone comes to you unexpectedly, it can be hard to respond with exactly what they need. Remember though they need to feel heard. Try:

    'That doesn't sound great, can you tell me more?'

- If you really are challenged with time, you could respond with

'That doesn't sound great. I want to understand this more and I am also conscious I have a piece of work I need to get done right now/a key meeting I need to attend. Can we have a cuppa (make it less formal and more relaxing) at x time? I know I can then give you my full attention. Our working relationship is important, so I want to know how I can best support to resolve this issue. In the meantime, what support do you have around you, to look after you?'

will support them, then you are more able to help them get curious about all the other perspectives of this situation. When you acknowledge to the other person, that your response wasn't ideal, it can strengthen the relationship.

After getting a conversation back on track after a less than ideal first reaction, it is important that you do reflect on what contributed to your initial reaction. What's the story in your head? What's a different narrative that better serves you and this person, as you work through this conflict?

We are all human. Don't be hard on yourself. Get curious about yourself. In every unhelpful reaction there is an opportunity for learning and growth which will help you in shrinking this elephant.

―――

Principle Three: Accept multiple truths

Your role, in elephant shrinking, is to unearth the stories that the involved parties have, both conscious and unconscious.

It is only through unearthing each other's stories and feeling validated for them, that people have a chance of getting curious about other perspectives of the elephant. This is needed, to resolve conflict.

While this book is focused on relationships in the workplace, I draw on the resources of experts in the field of relationships beyond the work environment, to help make sense of workplace behaviours. Esther Perel[*], a clinical psychologist, public speaker, and author, identifies that conflict in relationships is three sides of a triangle: power and control, support and care and respect and recognition. People create their own story about whether

---
[*] www.estherperel.com

FIGURE FOURTEEN

The underlying sources of conflict – our basic human needs

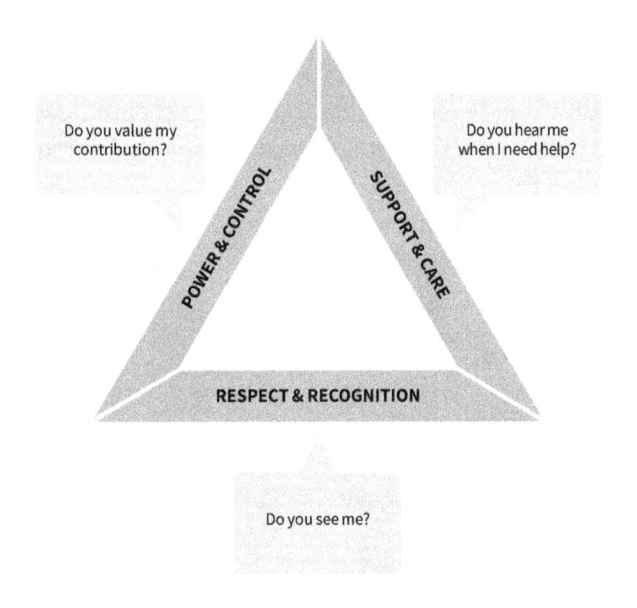

Triangle diagram with sides labeled POWER & CONTROL (left), SUPPORT & CARE (right), and RESPECT & RECOGNITION (bottom). Callouts: "Do you value my contribution?" (left), "Do you hear me when I need help?" (right), "Do you see me?" (bottom).

they are getting these. They are seeking answers to the questions: Do you see me? Do you value my contribution? Do you hear me when I need help? (Figure 14).

Everyone has their own version of the truth of this conflict which makes sense to them. Perel says we have 10 secs to breathe through something we completely disagree with, before we can't listen anymore because we are triggered. We don't feel in control. We don't feel respected. We don't feel supported. We feel this reaction, because of the lenses that we wear.

When others aren't curious about their lenses, you need to be. This is far easier said than done. Remember your brain hunts for pattern and has a confirmation bias. Once you start to form a view, of what has happened in a situation, you unconsciously seek information that supports that view. You are more likely to reject information as not relevant when it doesn't support your view, unless you remain curious.

When I was studying occupational therapy, I was introduced to the scientific research method by which you form a hypothesis of what you think you will find in the research. Then deliberately go looking for evidence to disprove that hypothesis. This was seen as a way of countering the bias the brain has. Keep remembering those lenses. You have them. Every single person in the conflict has them. They create truth on what is happening in this conflict for that person. When someone isn't curious, they can believe that they 'own the truth'. The more people who believe one truth over another, the more intense the conflict can get (see Figure 15). Your role is to stay curious. Be a caring scientist, to unearth these different truths, rather than just seeking information that supports your view of the conflict.

I had a team member, who was convinced I was avoiding them. One day, I was walking into our work area, realised I had left something in the last meeting room and headed back out. Completely unaware that this person was walking toward me. What did they see? Me coming into the work area, seeing them and turning away to avoid them. This was then translated back to me. I have illustrated this in Table 6, as a simple way of showing how your lenses influence your interpretation of a behaviour.

I realised how they were caught in their own cortisol pattern of threat. Using the Five components of understanding an elephant, we were able to get curious about each other's perspective. Connection then curiosity, enabled us to discuss what we both needed from each other, to work effectively together.

If you feel a greater affinity for one person over another, involved in the conflict, your ability to stay completely curious is further chal-

FIGURE FIFTEEN

But I own the truth!!

"I own the truth."

"No! I own the truth."

"Are you kidding! We own the truth!"

lenged. When you find someone who is easy to work with you will be naturally more forgiving of transgressions. You can easily buy into their perspective as being the 'right one'. When someone is harder to work with, you are more likely to be critical of their view and unconsciously be biased to look for evidence which disproves their view.

TABLE SIX

In conflict there is observable behaviour that is then given context by the lenses each person wears

What I did	Factual what anyone could observe	What they saw with a lens of 'she is ignoring me'
I walked into the work area, realised I had left something in the last meeting room and abruptly turned around and walked back out.	I walked into the work area then abruptly turned around and walked back out.	I walked into the work area, saw them and **abruptly turned around and walked back out** to avoid them.

There is never one truth – there are multiple truths depending on the lenses worn.

The aim is not to apportion blame when you are trying to work out how to resolve conflict. Rather, your role is to help those involved get curious, about where their own truth comes from. From there, they can start to appreciate where someone else's truth could come from. Even hard ones. In this way, people can then appreciate how they unintentionally contributed to the conflict. To then determine what practical things they could do, to resolve this now and learn for the future. You need to help those involved, to accept there are multiple truths.

As you start on this journey of elephant shrinking, I want you to become aware of when you slip into 'I know what is happening' as compared to 'I am listening to understand multiple truths' mode.

Principle Four: Balance your time

Embracing the curiosity of understanding multiple truths, does not mean endless questions. Action is needed.

> *You need to take the time to understand all the layers of the ecosystem, to help people triangulate, what the 3D elephant looks like. While not stretching on for so long, that people feel like you aren't taking any action.*

What I know from undertaking investigations over the years, is that our memories do not just fade, but rather morph over time. What we remember, when something happens and how we make sense of it or explain it, changes over time. It gets influenced by what we hear from others. How we connect the dots, through our own lenses, between this and other things that have occurred in our past. It is shaped by our animal brain, working to make sense of the pattern, so we can feel safe again. The first component of balancing time is to move reasonably quickly, before people get entrenched with stories in their head, that justifies their behaviour and vilifies the other person.

On the flip side of balancing time is moving too fast. Don't move so quickly to gather information, that you look like the hero 'solving' the issue but leave people feeling that they haven't been heard. In looking purely at a physical failure of a system, moving quickly to gather evidence is critical. But the moment you introduce the complexity of conflict between people, the perspective of time needs to shift. In conflict, there are more perspectives on 'the truth', than facts. There can be objective assessments of behaviours, if they are corroborated, such as
- They raised their voice.
- They walked out of the room.
- They didn't attend the meeting.

But beyond this, is a world of truths. You need to create the time to understand these truths, to get a triangulated, 3D version of the elephant.

How much time you take needs to be balanced out. Too fast and people won't feel heard. Too slow and people won't feel heard. There is risk either way. Be conscious of time and the impact of it. Balance your time.

Principle Five: Understand your role

The Chinese philosopher, Lao Tzu said:

'Give a man a fish and you feed him for a day. Teach him how to fish and you feed him for a lifetime'

This is so true when it comes to elephant shrinking. When you are in a management role, people expect you to 'get the job done'. Indeed, this is what you are accountable for. Your job may not be secure, without delivering. Many a manager thinks though that their only role is the task. To deliver the fish now. Forgetting, that if they want to deliver consistent, sustainable results, they need to step into juggling the three balls of leadership, task team and self (Figure 16), that teach the team *how* to fish.

When you think as a manager with one very large task ball, it is easy to fall into the mode of 'getting things done' in which you direct others. Don't get me wrong. In the context of leading, there are decisions you need to make and directives you need to give, to move forward. There is a difference though, between making a captain's call in a particular situation and getting hooked into

FIGURE SIXTEEN

Shifting from a management to leadership perspective

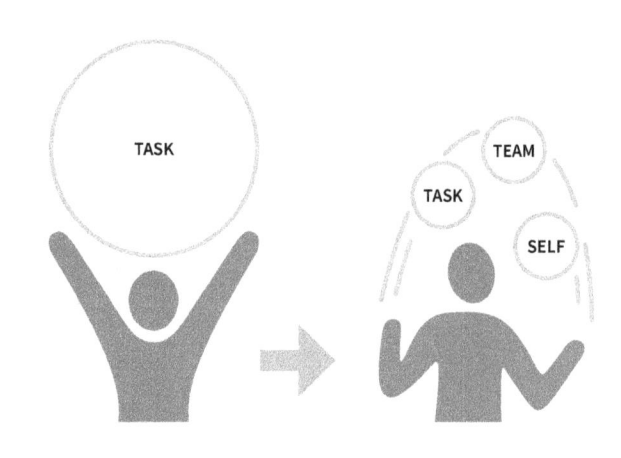

being a hero. Being hooked into being a hero is not bringing out the best in others.

Being a hero is addictive. You feel valued. Directing, gets things done quickly. 'Rescuing' others, can feel satisfying. You feel like you are genuinely making a difference. You need to beware in conflict though, that being the one 'with the answers' isn't the answer. You want to build capability in people to recognise their own and others' stories, therefore lenses. This is what enables them to shrink elephants and choose together how to move forward. You need to step back from the advice-giving hero and become a caring scientist, to help people shrink the elephant and therefore resolve conflict.

'Your advice steals my learning'*

---

* Anagnostakis, A. (2023). Is Giving Advice Helping Others' Vertical Development or Stealing Their Learning? Vertical Development Institute: How Grown-Ups Grow Up. Substack. 13th July 2023.

Your team needs to learn how to fish. Not being a hero, starts early on in a conflict situation. Particularly if someone comes to you to complain about another person's behaviour. A response of 'I'll speak to them to sort it out' or 'I'll speak to their manager' is not helpful. You may have even done this yourself, in the past. It is easy to do. You hear your team member's perspective, and it sounds reasonable. You think reminding someone else to be reasonable, will solve it. But flip the shoe for a moment. Imagine if you think things are going along well. Then your own manager comes to you and says, 'I have some feedback that you have been doing x, which isn't appropriate'. Your animal brain will spike with cortisol. Do you think your reaction to this unexpected third-party feedback will then be productive? It likely won't. Your role when someone comes to you to complain is to help them have the conversation they need to have with the other person, not solve it for them. Teach them how to fish.

> *Stepping in to have the conversation, that other parties need to have with each other, is allowing them to avoid discomfort, and limiting their growth potential.*

When you are working to shrink your own elephant, continue to refrain from giving the other person involved, advice. Own your own role. Use connection and curious questions, to help them understand their role. Regardless of their reporting line, in relation to you, help them learn how to fish.

You have experience and wisdom. Yes, you can help. But you don't have all the answers. You hold one of many perspectives of the elephant. Yes, it might be broader than others, but not necessarily complete. Your role is to help everyone, including yourself, triangulate the stories that come out, to get the 3D perspective of the elephant, which shrinks it to a manageable size.

PRACTICAL STEPS:

Not being a hero: Helping someone have the conversation they need to have

The first step in not being a hero is to remember these questions when someone complains to you about someone else's behaviour:

- Have you had a conversation with them about this situation? If not, what is getting in your way? How can I help you prepare to have that conversation with them?
- If you have tried and it hasn't worked, have you told them you were going to speak to me about the situation? Have you invited them to join you? If not, how can I help you prepare to have that conversation with them?
- If they said yes to those questions and the other person has refused to join, then you can start getting curious. What is going on for them? What do they think is going on for the other person? What is stopping them from choosing to shrink the elephant? Your role is to then get the other person to the table.
- Your role still isn't to solve the conflict. It is to help the people involved develop the skills to solve the conflict themselves by hearing each other. By helping them have the conversation with each other directly, not via you, you are teaching them how to fish.
- Own your own conversations. Where you are feeling the direct impact of conflict yourself with another person, have a direct conversation. Visibly role modelling owning your conversations helps others own theirs.
- You can be present to facilitate conversations (see Chapter 6 for more on this), but don't enable others to avoid the conversations they need to have.
- The one exception to gently holding people to account to have the conversation themselves is where you see clear evidence of bullying/harassment i.e. clearly unacceptable behaviour.

THE FIVE PRINCIPLES OF SHRINKING AN ELEPHANT

Key things to remember

Conflict can be seen as complex. If you have avoided it in the past or stepped in, and it hasn't been resolved, it can make you feel somewhat uncomfortable about wanting to step in at all. There is so much wasted energy in workplaces though, because of both quiet and loud conflict. Everyone, including you, wear lenses that give a perspective on the world. Everyone is doing the best they can with what they have. Helping people see the full 3D elephant, from all its different perspectives, is what shrinks the elephant to a manageable size for them. When you can accept the full picture, it isn't as insurmountable as you might have thought. Use the principles from this chapter, to make elephant shrinking less daunting.

Remember:
1. **Safety comes first:** When the brain is under threat, the chemicals override everything. ALL parties need to feel supported, including you. How will you elicit the oxytocin and serotonin needed throughout the process for others? And who does that for you?
2. **Initial reactions count:** Your initial reaction to others who are in conflict, will significantly influence the outcome. Keep practising that deep breath before you respond. Practice a warm and curious initial response.
3. **Accept multiple truths:** Stay curious to the situation and to yourself. There is no one truth in conflict – just a variety of perspectives. Everyone is biased including you! Recognise when you think you know the answers. Look for alternative perspectives, until everyone can agree on the triangulated 3D elephant to move forward with.
4. **Balance your time:** Don't speed. Don't take too long. Take the right time to help people feel heard by each other and by you.

5. **Understand your role:** Your role isn't to 'solve' it for others. Your role is to own your part and build the curiosity muscle in all parties, in a safe environment. This is about helping now *and* building long term skills for all involved.

In all of this, you must believe it is worth the time, to get uncomfortable with what the reactions might tell you about yourself. This is lifelong learning. Help others, by stepping into any discomfort that arises and see the opportunity to unlock potential in yourself.

Now you have understood the benefit of elephant shrinking, you have the right support around you, and you are familiar with the elephant shrinking principles, the next chapter enables you to shrink persistent elephants, before they grow to an unwieldy size.

CHAPTER SIX

LET'S SHRINK AN ELEPHANT

'What if you were wrong?'[*]

This chapter will be focused on those elephants that have started to obviously interfere with getting work done. Where they haven't been shrunk by those directly involved. Where the conflict is no longer quiet and you are stepping in as a leader, to help resolve it. It will cover:
- The layers of causation – getting to root cause, when you are not a psychologist.
- Staying connected AND curious throughout, when you want it closed out quickly.
- The role of restorative justice in moving forward.

---

[*] Grant, A. (2023). Think Again: The Power of Knowing what you Don't Know. W H Allen. UK.

- Applying 'restorative justice' in practice.
- Recognising when you do need more structured help outside the team.
- The nuance when you yourself are directly involved in the conflict.

As you embark on helping people to understand and shrink elephants, keep in mind the importance of natural justice. People have the right to be heard. To be treated without bias. To have decisions based on relevant, clear evidence. Through this chapter, you will learn how to help people feel heard, through the way you approach each conversation. How to stay curious to avoid your own bias. How to work collectively to make decisions on the way forward. Keep testing your approach through the lens of 'How would I feel about this approach being used with me if I was feeling vulnerable or threatened? Am I treating people fairly?'

Getting to the root cause of conflict

In this section I am going to draw on my experiences in leading safety investigations, for considering how far to go with question asking. It has long been ingrained in me, that if you don't understand the root causes (and to be clear there is never one sole root cause), then all you do is put a band aid on an infected wound. A common response I would see from managers, when a serious incident occurred, is defence of the organisation/themselves with a view that 'the person did the wrong thing'. I understand why this initial conclusion is drawn by many. A belief that the systems of work were safe. A desire to get on with the 'real' work at hand. The difficulty in seeing the ecosystem in which people operate.

All this can limit how far the questioning goes. The outcome then becomes educating/coaching the person, to 'do the right thing'. People don't go to work to deliberately do the wrong thing though. Like that infected wound with a band-aid over it, all looks ok. A box is ticked, and you go on with work. But when that infection comes back, it comes back with a vengeance. It could be through more serious incidents. Or conflict and performance issues with the person, because their own anger bubbles up at being blamed. They get frustrated when you are not asking the questions, that face into work demands and what the culture drives in people's behaviour.

Use the principle of balancing your time, in considering how deep you go. Thinking too simplistically doesn't get to the stories that are circulating in people's heads. At the other end of the spectrum though is, the risk of analysis paralysis. You can feel like you are getting too far away from the issue at hand. You need to spend the right time to understand the elephant from multiple perspectives.

While I have been exposed to a range of investigative techniques in my career, the simplest and most effective I have found is the 'Five Why's'. That is, for each question answered, you are asking 'why did that happen?' The idea being, by the time you get to that fifth 'why', you are at a much deeper layer of system understanding. I have changed from starting a question with 'why' because people can become defensive and blame others. Rather I lead with, 'Help me understand what led to that decision?' Or 'Help me understand what led to that event?' Or a variation on this. Five times. Don't take that literally. Sometimes, at four, you can both see the 3D elephant start to emerge. Sometimes, it takes just a little bit more of a nudge with another couple of rounds of this question. Sometimes remaining silent, but warm and curious, after the initial question, provides the opportunity for the person to really open up. Each time you get an answer, you go to a deeper layer of understanding the 3D elephant.

Here is a simple example:

What happened?	*We have made the wrong decision about X.*
Help me understand, what led to that?	*Incomplete information was in the report that the decision was based on.*
Help me understand, what led to that?	*We were under time pressure to get the report out.*
Help me understand what led to that?	*The timeframe got moved up, because we needed the decision made before you went on holidays.*
Help me understand what led to the decision to not raise the timeframe with me?	*I didn't appreciate the significance of the missing information, because I didn't have the time to check it.*
Help me understand what led to you not feeling comfortable with raising the timeframe?	*Our manager has made it clear it is our role to make sure we hit deadlines. I have seen the impact on others, when they don't.*

One conversation doesn't get you to the full answer. However, this starts to reveal where you want to explore more:
- What is happening in the ecosystem, that leads a manager to believe that deadlines always come before quality?
- What is happening in the ecosystem, that leads people to not speak up, when requests are unreasonable?

I remember being asked to investigate a particularly sensitive major incident, that had occurred for an international client. Luckily, no one had been injured. The collapse of a major part of a new production line clearly indicated there were issues to be resolved. It was that critical, that I needed to brief the global Managing Director, at the end of each day. I had engineers looking at the actual physical structures. I was leading the interviews with those involved. In the first day, I had some great conversations with people who were calm, confident and very believable in their responses to what caused the collapse. Indeed, it created a consistent story. In my brief at the end of day one, I gave insights that were consistent with this. Management was satisfied with the initial conclusions drawn. On day two of the interviews, I started to hear different stories. Stories that challenged the perspectives from day one. So, in my update on day two, I flagged that new evidence was coming in. That we all needed to keep an open mind on the contributing causes. That I needed to go back to talk to those I spoke to on day 1. This continued through the 5 days. I would hear multiple different perspectives. And who was right? All of them. Because this was their reality. Their perspective of the elephant. It was only through continuing to use the 'Five Whys', that I could understand the whole elephant. Presenting back to senior management on all the layers that led to this incident. Management had a very different understanding of the elephant at the beginning and the end, through me being able to identify multiple root causes, using this questioning approach.

Ultimately how far you go with asking questions of those involved, will depend on the situation at hand. Keeping the elephant shrinking principles in mind, the next section takes you through those first conversations. Conversations that are critical to seeing the different angles on the elephant. In accepting multiple truths.

PRACTICAL STEPS:
Getting to the root cause of conflict
Never underestimate the power of asking:

'Help me understand, what led to that decision/event?'

Five times. To each person involved in the conflict.

Am I staying connected while I learn about the elephant?

Prioritising people over process is important to stay connected. Here are some pointers for that first conversation with a key player involved in the conflict.

Establish a sense of connection up front: What do you have in common that you can laugh about? Keep eye contact. Reassure you want to help everyone understand what the issues are and how to collectively solve them. All of this should be done with warmth, to do your best to elicit some oxytocin at the start.

It is also useful to acknowledge, that one of the things you have in common, is that this is an uncomfortable situation. They need to feel like you have their back. This is another reason why you don't want an HR person at this point. They don't have the person's back per se, as they don't have the long-term relationship. Getting the person to laugh, smile or at the least, make good eye contact, is important.

Explain your approach and ask for permission to take some notes to help remember. This helps their pattern seeking brain see what the pathway is for the next short period of time. This is all about

managing cortisol levels as much as you can. I would suggest that the approach you explain is:
- You want to spend no more than an hour with them. (It is always good to set a time limit for their own pattern seeking brain.) Your focus is to make sure you understand their perspective.
- Then you want to explore with them who else might be valuable to chat to.
- Set an expectation that you will come back more than once to talk through your evolving understand of the elephant. Then, at some point, will get all parties together. It is important that they are clear up front, that while no one loves conflict, the ability to talk effectively through it, will really strengthen the relationships. Your aim is to facilitate a mutual understanding.
- **Reinforce connection throughout.** Remember that animal brain. They will keep getting cortisol spikes. You need to keep flooding them with oxytocin and serotonin. Make good eye contact. Listen not just to what they are saying, but what they aren't saying. Tune into their body language.

Useful questions:
- *Tell me from your perspective what happened.* This is about helping them feel heard.
- *How did that make you feel then? How are you feeling now?* This is about helping them feel seen. It also gives you some great insights into how threatened they feel. Demonstrate empathy. You may think their response is irrational. It may well be. But being able to say 'that's a tough space to be in' can help them feel seen. Remember, you need to balance out their cortisol with some oxytocin and serotonin. Then, they can more clearly articulate their view of the elephant. It is only when they get curious, because their brain is feeling more balanced, that they can start being part of the solution.

- You then go into the **'Five Whys'** of **'Help me understand what led to that decision/event'**
- *What do you think contributed to the person behaving this way?* This is helping them start to shift perspective. This is unearthing the story they are telling themselves about the elephant. I do love the question 'so what is the story you have in your head about what is going on here?' but people can become defensive at that question. So 'what do you think is going on for the other person' is a more comfortable way through.
- *What would you have liked them to have done instead? And if they had done that, what would you feel about them and the situation?* This is also about you getting some insights into how this person is thinking. How their emotions are influencing them. What lenses they are wearing.
- *What do you think could be the perspectives from the other person?* I love the question 'How might you be wrong?' Or 'what other explanation could there be for that behaviour?' This is about challenging a pattern seeking brain to look for a different pattern. But again, like 'what's the story in your head' that can be confronting. This is a gentler way in.
- *What else can you see has contributed to the conflict?* This helps you to start sensing the impact of the broader ecosystem.

It is valuable at this point to reflect. To help this person feel like you have heard them. It can be useful to use the following frame for this:
- *What I have heard, is you experienced...*
- *And this had you feeling...*
- *You believe that this was caused by...*
- *And to move forward you would like the other person to...*
- *Have I captured that accurately?*
- *In an ideal world, what would you see are the valuable steps to take from here?*

This is where you need to start bringing your judgement in. Remember principle one, 'Safety First Always'. You need them to build up their elephant shrinking muscles. You also can't possibly know what is happening across the entire ecosystem, without talking to others (and examining your own lenses in the process). Consider closing the conversation with:
- *How do you feel? What support do you need right now?*
- *What are you comfortable owning yourself right now to do?* Agree on those actions. Sometimes, this one conversation unlocks something for that person. They then decide to have a next conversation themselves. What is important though, is that each person leaves the conversation, with an active role to play. Not a passive one. It could be them reflecting on what the alternative perspectives could be. Or thinking about their own mental health pie.* What actions do they need to take to look after themselves?

Confirm process from here: Who you will chat to. A timeframe to come back to them.

Close out with connection: Eye contact and even a hand to the upper arm or their hand (depending on your relationship and their comfort) reassures them that you value them.

---

* Hawkins, G. (2020). Mentally at Work: Optimising Health and Business Performance through Connection. Mentally at Work. Melbourne, Australia.

PRACTICAL STEPS:

A conversation to understand an elephant from one person's perspective

- Establish a sense of connection up front.
- Explain your approach.
- Reinforce connection throughout.
- Confirm where to from here at the end.

Useful questions for the conversation:

- *Tell me from your perspective what happened?*
- *How did that make you feel then? How are you feeling now?*
- *Help me understand what led to that decision/event.*
- *What do you think contributed to the person behaving this way?*
- *What would you have liked them to have done instead? And if they had done that, what would you feel about them and the situation?*
- *What do you think could be the perspectives from the other person?*
- *What else can you see has contributed to the conflict?*

Reflect:

- *What I have heard is you experienced…*
- *And this had you feeling…*
- *You believe that this was caused by…*
- *And to move forward you would like the other person to…*
- *Have I captured that accurately?*
- *In an ideal world, what would you see are the valuable steps to take from here?*
- *How do you feel? What support do you need right now?*
- *What are you comfortable owning yourself right now to do?*

All first conversations are different because everyone's lenses are different. Here are some typical challenges with this first conversation and how you might address them:

- **They may be so angry or upset, that the emotions are flooding them, and they can't think clearly.** Give them the space and silence to allow them to say what they can. Ask them how they feel. (Don't assume you know. There is always nuance.) Acknowledge that it is hard. Ask them if they need to take a break. Just sit with them quietly, as their emotion literally works its way through the body. (Do make sure the room isn't one where anyone could walk by and see them become emotional). You also need to make a judgement call on time. As a general principle, stick to the maximum hour. If you get to the half hour mark and they are still emotional, and you can clearly see an hour won't be enough, suggest to them that you help them find the right support for now and start again later.
- **They have limited to no insight.** These people tend to blame everyone else and not themselves. There is always a justification for their behaviour being caused by others. What this means is they have too much cortisol in their system. You won't get them curious in one chat. Be patient. Focus on decreasing cortisol. Get a bit of oxytocin and serotonin coming in. Validate through reflecting back with 'what I hear is you experienced x, and you feel y. Have I understood you accurately?' Remember, they are doing the best they can with what they have. Thank them for the insights they provided. Don't push them to explore other alternatives straight away. You want them to walk out of the conversation trusting you.
- **You find yourself getting frustrated.** Can you take a deep breath in the moment? Or do you need to call it and say, 'I recognise while I wanted to have this conversation now, that I am not as fully present as I want to be. Can we just take a 5 min pause?' Consider rescheduling if you need a longer break.

PRACTICAL STEPS:

Variation on the theme of useful questions to understand an elephant from your peer's/Manager's perspective

'It feels like there is an elephant between us. I am wondering if we could perhaps talk through what might be happening. I would love to understand your perspective, so I can appreciate the impact on you. Then reflect on my experience, so we can work out a more productive way forward. Does that sound ok?'

'Can I understand from your perspective what you saw happened?'

'How did that impact you?'

'What are your assumptions on why I behaved this way?'

'What would you have preferred me to do? And if I had done that, what would you feel about me and the situation?'

'What I have heard is you experienced...'
- *'And this had you feeling...'*
- *'You believe that this was caused by...'*
- *'And to move forward you would prefer it if I...'*
- *'Have I captured that accurately?'*

'I appreciate your honesty in helping me understand your perspective and the impact of my behaviour. I am sorry it had that impact. Perhaps not surprisingly, I experienced this differently. Can I share my experience?'

'I agree with your observations that I did...(confirm the common ground on observable behaviour)'

'What I had observed prior was...

'This story in my head was...

'This had me feeling...

'My intention was...

'I can understand how you could have interpreted my behaviour in the way you explained. What other questions would you like to ask me to better understand my perspective?'

'So, it feels like:
- despite our differences we now agree on...'
- and we still have some things to still work through on...'

'In an ideal world, what would you see are the valuable steps for us to take from here?'

Regardless of who you are having the conversation with, stay aware of the risk that you find yourself confident you know what has caused it and how to solve it. You are likely caught in bias and stepping into hero mode. Let's look at that specifically in this next section.

Are you staying curious?

The moment you start thinking you have the right perspective, and you just need to convince others of this, is a red flag that you have lost your curiosity to the multiple truths.

In being a caring scientist, ask yourself:
- Am I eliciting oxytocin and serotonin in those involved?
- Do they feel heard? Can they identify the lenses they are wearing?
- Have I got them curious, to understand the other person's story?
- Am I remaining warm and curious?
- What am I missing?

PRACTICAL STEPS:
Staying curious

- Can you accept that you have unconscious lenses that influence your perspective?
- Sounds simple but put a sticky note on your computer or in your diary or as a task reminder that comes up in your phone calendar every hour or so (or every day for longer enquiries) that says 'Accept multiple truths'. That regular visual is a good circuit breaker for your brain.
- Each time you find yourself drawing a conclusion, ask yourself 'how might I be wrong?' Then seek evidence that supports you are wrong so you can accept multiple truths about the elephant.
- You aren't looking for the 'right' answer, you are looking for people to feel heard. For people to see a 3D elephant. To agree on a way forward. Keep checking in with those involved. Do they feel heard? Can they describe this 3D elephant? Can they start to see a way forward?
- You will naturally develop beliefs and perspectives and judgements on others. The risk is not that this will happen. It is inevitable. The risk is that you think you are right about this perspective. Quick judgements of others, however, say more about you and your lenses, rather than the actual situation. When you see your own judgements bubble up, see this as a great opportunity to learn more about yourself and your own lenses. Ask yourself, what might be an alternative truth?
- Sometimes you may need some help when your own emotions and related stories are getting in the way. Check in with your Board regularly to help them hold you to account for staying curious to the multiple truths.

What is restorative justice?

Let's jump forward now. At this point, you have some reasonable clarity on how each person is currently describing the elephant. Therefore, what lenses they might be wearing. You have got them curious enough to think about what success looks like for them, moving forward. Hopefully, you have also got them thinking about the idea of what a different take on this situation might be. What you now need to do is bring the parties together. It is only through bringing them together, that they can find a way to truly feel heard and move forward. This next step is about each person feeling that the way forward feels 'right' to them.

I was first exposed to the concept of a just and fair culture and restorative justice, in the context of health and safety and the Workers' Compensation arena. In looking at helping someone recover from whatever injury they sustained at work, they needed to feel that the right changes had happened. This acknowledged their pain. It helped them move on. In the legal arena in victims of crime, the focus is to help those who have been harmed, to heal. Restorative justice provides an opportunity for the 'offender', to communicate with the 'victim' and take responsibility, for the harm caused. In both Workers' Compensation and in the criminal process, restorative justice enables the person impacted to feel heard.

> *'Words of apology, no matter how sincere, will not heal a broken connection if we haven't listened well to the hurt party's anger and pain.'*[*]

If an individual doesn't feel understood and supported, no matter what others say, they will get stuck in a chronic flight/fight/freeze/

---

[*] Lerner, H. PhD. (2017). Why Won't You Apologize? Healing Big Betrayals and Everyday Hurts. Duckworth Overlook. London, UK.

fawn cycle. That is, they will see patterns that keep spiking cortisol in their brain.

The challenge in conflict, is that all parties involved are the 'offender' AND the 'victim'.

Each person needs the other person, to play the role of offender. Acknowledging their hurt and pain. The question becomes, how can you help them both acknowledge each other's story, when each expects the other to make the first move?

Cast your mind back to a situation where you felt hard done by. I am sure you can remember a moment. Your emotions got stuck in irritation/annoyance/hurt or whatever it may be. Someone wasn't acknowledging your perspective as valid. It may have been a performance rating you didn't agree with. A bonus you thought you were getting and didn't get. A promotion or job you didn't receive. Unjustified criticism of work you delivered. You could also think of home. An argument where you felt the other person was the unreasonable one. Someone didn't do what they said they would do. There are countless times when you can experience not feeling seen and heard. Recall how you felt. Consider that the other person had a different story to you and were irate at your response. How capable would you have been to fully listen to the other person, accept their position and apologise for your impact, when you were feeling your intense emotions?

To enable restorative justice, you need to be the leader who helps the parties involved truly feel heard and safe <u>with you</u>.

Then you can gauge, who might be the best person, to listen to the other person's story, first. Your role as a leader, is to help these people build trust between them, to move forward. Don't think about this as 'let's all say sorry and move on'. This is about those involved coming to terms with and accepting multiple truths. Acknowledging their own contribution. Then agreeing on a way forward together.

Dealing with issues behind closed doors with a 'Thanks, we are dealing with it, please get on with your work', doesn't cut it, in effectively shrinking the elephant. In fact, it can do the opposite. It can cause it to grow even more, for those locked out of the room. This is ignoring principle five, 'Understand your Role'. This isn't what restorative justice is about. People need to be heard. They need to be in the driver's seat to move forward. There are too many cases, where the action from an investigation, is that one person needs to do some learning. Perhaps a refresher on a code of conduct. With the complainant left in the dark and told to move on. This isn't what helps people move forward. Both people learning about their own and each other's stories is the way forward.

When restorative justice is applied effectively in conflict, the parties involved can move through the phases of: I feel heard; I now hear and understand the other person; I own my part; they own theirs; we have agreed on a way forward that works for both of us.

Each step must be worked through one by one. You can't pass go and move to the next step, without the prior one being achieved (Figure 17).

FIGURE SEVENTEEN

The phrases of restorative justice in conflict

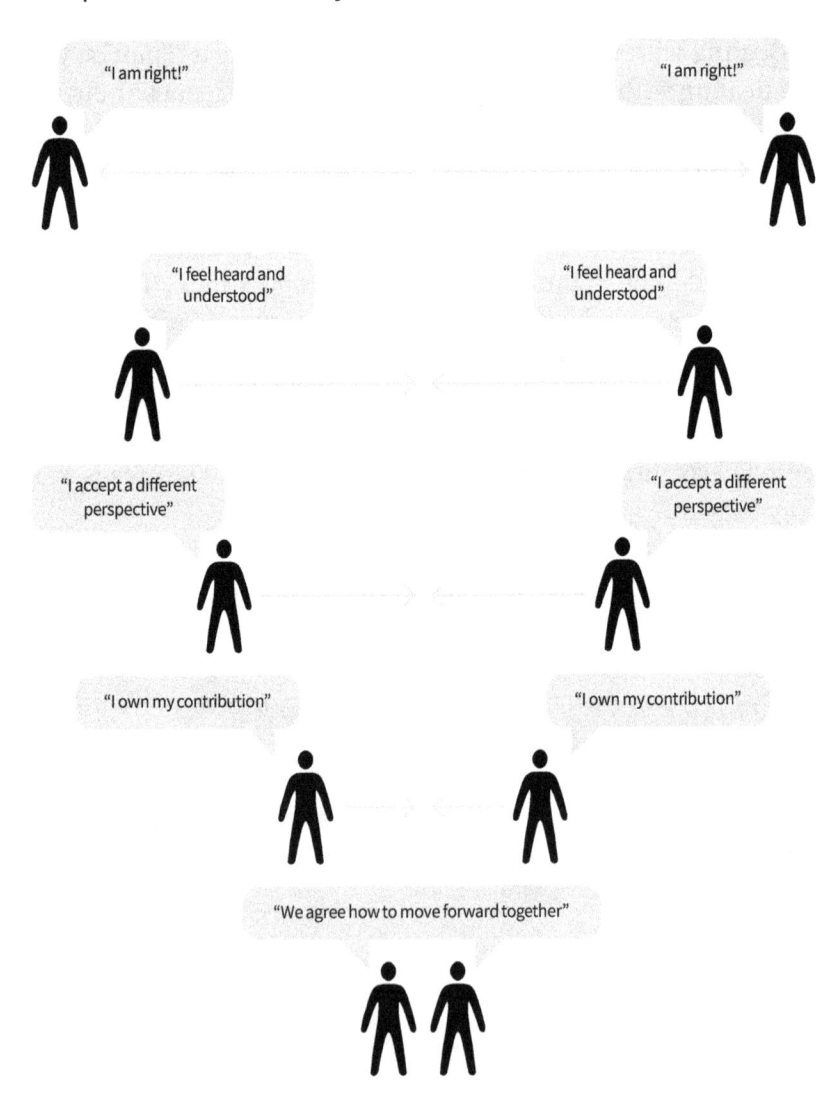

"I am right!"

"I am right!"

"I feel heard and understood"

"I feel heard and understood"

"I accept a different perspective"

"I accept a different perspective"

"I own my contribution"

"I own my contribution"

"We agree how to move forward together"

Restorative justice in practice

Below, is a guide for how you might frame up a conversation on next steps. Importantly, through these conversations, you need to consistently demonstrate your support and curiosity. Demonstrate your own ability to hear and change perspective. Take ownership for what you can do differently.

Here's a suggestion on how to get started

> *'I want to thank you for your active involvement in this. I appreciate it isn't easy having these uncomfortable conversations. What I do believe though, is that these situations can help all of us to grow. When I have reflected on this situation, there are things I have learnt about my own lenses. How this shapes my actions as a leader. These include… (Insert your own insights into yourself here. This sets the stage for vulnerability from others). What I also know is that we all wear these different lenses. You have been great at articulating your own perspective on the situation and generous in what you think might be going on for the other person. What I would like to do, is get both of you together; to help you both listen and understand each other's perspectives. How would you feel about this?'*

Depending on their reaction you might need to ask,

> *'What would you need in place to feel safe in talking about this together?'*

Sometimes, this might be about who is present in the room. It can also be the person most deeply impacted going first, in explaining their story. Responses to this may mean you go back and forth a couple of times. To agree on what is in place for safety, to then be able to listen to each other. This may include talking to the person who is going second, on what they might need to do. To help them stay in a listening, not defensive mode, during the conversation. You also want to help them prepare for the sharing of their story. Ask them to write down their story, using the Five Components of understanding an elephant from two different perspectives that you learnt in Chapter 3.

- When we were doing… (situation).
- I noticed… (behaviour explanation).
- The story in my head was…(remember this is critical, that they own they have only one of multiple truths here, based on their lenses).
- This story has me feeling… (impact – again critical that they are able to identify what they are feeling).
- I recognise that there could be a different perspective. I would like to hear your story/how your story is different to mine (depending on who goes first).

Once you have them both together, work to get some oxytocin into their brains. Regardless of what they say, they will both have a level of nerves about the conversation, that triggers cortisol. Their brains are on the lookout for where an attack might come from. If you can elicit some laughter from them to begin with, it's amazing what that can achieve. For example, you might start with 'I know we have a serious conversation to explore here but I just wanted to share something funny that happened to me' (might be a pet/child/clumsy story). This is about both reminding them you are a safe human, and that this environment is safe. Then you want to set out what the plan is:

> 'We can all acknowledge there has been some discomfort here, that hasn't been able to be resolved. I have appreciated what you have both done in being willing to be here together today. What I want to do is help both of you listen to each other's stories. Then, you can work out what you can both own moving forward, to strengthen this important relationship, between the two of you. I want x to go first then y to go second. What I need both of you to do, is listen to what the other person is saying. Then reflect what you have heard, to see if we can get a common understanding of the elephant. Then we can explore what's next.'

During the conversation, observe how both parties are approaching it. Are they maintaining eye contact? Do they appear to be actively listening? Can you see cortisol creeping in? How well are they reflecting? What you are working to do here, is develop their skills and their relationship with each other. You may need to coach along the way. It can be useful to use language such as...

> 'I would like us to pause for a moment. I am noticing… (Name the unhelpful behaviour). Could we all take a deep breath and focus on… (desired behaviour) as we continue the conversation.'

It may take more than one conversation, for those involved, to be able to listen to each other effectively.

Once you have helped them hear each other's stories, ask them to reflect on what they have learned about themselves, in this process. Depending on the situation, you may suggest having a break and coming back to this next phase. This will be dependent on the size of the elephant you are trying to understand. Ideally, you have caught it early enough that you can move now into finding agreement on the way forward. So, you ask each person:

> *'What have you learnt about yourself through this conflict that will help you in future situations?*
>
> *Moving forward, what can you do differently to help decrease this social friction?*
>
> *What would you love the other person to do?*
>
> *What could you do to help the other person if they find that hard?'*

Reflect what you have heard. Then ask:

> *'Having heard all this, what are you committing to?'*

You then want each person to be able to say:
- I own my lenses and recognise how they create the stories and emotions that bubble up.
- I can see we have common ground in that we both…
- I have learnt… about myself through this.
- I am taking ownership by doing…
- I can appreciate the other person is owning their part too in what they will do.
- I recognise what I can control and will focus on that.

It is then important to acknowledge, we can all have the best of intentions, but we can easily slip up. So, ask each of them:

> *'What can be a simple way of you acknowledging when you have slipped up, to reassure the other person you will keep working on it?*

'What can be a simple way of letting the other person know when they have slipped? How could you encourage them to keep going with their commitment, rather than criticise them?'

Accept you are both human. You will make mistakes. Being a supporter of helping each other grow, is so important to truly strengthen the relationship. I was once leading a team where I recognised that I could sometimes get too intense in the way I was asking questions of the team. This was always with good intent, with a brain that often had multiple tabs open. I wanted to help people get the best result. This however, had the potential and did end up causing some people to feel uncomfortable. I acknowledged to the team what I was working to improve in my approach. One of the simple ways I asked for help from the team, in holding me to account, was sending me an emoji of a dancing girl, if they felt I was slipping. It was such an easy circuit breaker. Asking them to do that, helped me be far more conscious of my behaviour. To the point I would ask one or two of them after a meeting whether perhaps I needed a dancing girl emoji. The ability to give this honest, supportive feedback continued to build these relationships of trust and keep me aware of this lens.

Examples of restorative commitments could be:
- Regular check-ins together on a weekly basis for the first few weeks to test any unhelpful stories creeping back in.
- One or both sharing their own leadership learning through the process with the broader team.
- One person may need to commit to some coaching support.
- Direct apologies to those impacted.
- Changes to process, or workload.
- Redefined accountabilities.
- Commitment to use the 5 components of understanding an elephant, earlier on.

The challenge in talking through this process, is that every situation has its nuances. Sometimes one person does need to take on greater commitments to change. Their lenses could be so thick, they don't have an appreciation of what they need to own. In these cases, you might choose to work with them first to help

PRACTICAL STEPS:
A restorative justice conversation
1. Help each person frame their perspective of the elephant in writing so they can practise it and even read from it if need be:
   a. When we were doing… (situation).
   b. I saw… (behaviour explanation).
   c. The story in my head was… (remember this is critical that they own they have only one of the perspectives here based on their lenses).
   d. This story has me feeling… (impact – again critical that they are able to identify what they are actual feeling).
   e. I recognise that there could be a different perspective. I would like to hear your story/how your story is different to mine (depending on who goes first).
2. Start the conversation with a focus on connection.
3. Watch throughout – Are people responding as if they are being heard and understood or do you need to take a moment to help shake off a cortisol build up?
4. Questions to ask after stories have been heard:
   a. What have you learnt about yourself through this conflict that will help you in future situations?
   b. Moving forward, what can you do differently to help decrease this social friction?
   c. What would you love the other person to do?
   d. What could you do to help the other person if they find that hard?

5. Help them to each summarise at the end with:
   a. I own my lenses and recognise how they create the stories and emotions that bubble up.
   b. I can see we have common ground in that we both…
   c. I have learnt… about myself through this.
   d. I am taking ownership by doing…
   e. I can appreciate the other person is owning their part too in what they will do.
   f. I recognise what I can control and will focus on that.
6. Talk about how to manage the setbacks:
   a. What can be a simple way of you acknowledging when you have slipped up, to reassure the other person you will keep working on it?
   b. What can be a simple way of letting the other know when they have slipped? How could you encourage them to keep going with their commitment rather than criticise them?

them get their head around what is needed. Likewise, regardless of your perspective on a situation, another person's own past trauma can have them feeling intense hurt, well beyond the context of the situation at hand. When you recognise one person is really struggling, don't force them to get together, rather seek help.

How do I recognise if I need more help?

Experience tells me, that focusing on the actions from Chapters 1–3 and then if more serious, the actions in Chapters 4–6, you will be able to face and create opportunity, from more than 80% of the elephants that arise. There are times however, when further support is needed. This may be because of what is presented up front or what emerges during the conversations. The 20% that need help include:
- Formal accusation of bullying and harassment.
- Formal accusation of sexual harassment.
- Clear evidence of breach of code of conduct or contractual obligations.
- Serious injury/illness.
- A Workers' Compensation claim has been lodged.
- Lawyers already engaged by one or more parties.
- Quickly deteriorating relationships during performance management.
- Complete 'stalemate' between peers.

There is a balancing act you need to play, in seeking help. If you pull in formal help too quickly, you can cause the parties involved to move even further apart. On the other hand, sometimes you need someone with a different set of lenses to you. To help people effectively reduce their cortisol, see their lenses, and get curious on a way forward. You need to make a judgement call on your own cortisol levels, to determine what help is needed in these circumstances. You aren't a trained mediator. You are a leader, with a role to help people learn and grow. You want to create a place where problem solving works well. If you are confident, you can resolve it, focus on that, with or without background support. The one exception is if there is clear evidence right from the start of sexual harassment, bullying or serious misconduct. You will need to seek help straight away for these situations. For these cases, please jump to Chapter 7. But sometimes it doesn't become clear straight away when you might need help. Let's explore when to ask for help.

In considering what help is needed, there can be a range of options including:
- Calling on one or more of your own 'Board' members to reflect with/manage your own emotions.
- Asking one or all parties, to access their own Board member.
- Asking one or more parties to bring their Board member to a conversation with you.
- Using someone skilled at facilitating these types of conversations (internally or externally).
- Accessing your HR account manager for general guidance, formal investigation, or legal advice.

Sometimes the help you need is a silent partner of support. That is, you feel safer because you have that coach in the background, helping you to choose the right path. The person/people directly involved don't need to know you have them. Sometimes though, you will need to pull the person into a formal process. My recommendation when you are feeling like you need support, is to start with who is on your Board. For more technical advice start with HR. If there are signs of ill health involved, start with a health and wellbeing advisor (if you have one in your organisation). These key people can help you to make that decision, on when to shift to a more formal process. Use Table 7 to guide you further in this decision.

Sometimes someone independent, but very skilled in developing rapport and facilitating conversations, can help you and others involved, to gain perspective. You want them to use this methodology, just independently. No formal report. Just an expe-

TABLE SEVEN

What support is valuable when?

Situation	Informal support	More formal support
Performance management.	Who is on your Board? This may include a P&C partner in the background to debrief after each conversation. For the most part, this is all you may need unless you have moved to termination stage.	Move to more formal HR support where termination could be a likely outcome from the process. Follow the formal HR process in your organisation. You may then choose to have an HR person present for conversations where you are concerned about how the other person is coping. Don't go to this immediately though as this can be intimidating. Ask their permission to do this and explain why. Who do they choose to have in the room for their support?
The person/people involved are not able to regulate their own emotions.	Access to someone who is an expert in this area can be valuable. They can give you tips on how to help the person take a deep breath, recognise their own emotion and respond differently. EAP providers may provide this service.	You may want to request the person bring a support person along to help them. Acknowledge it can be hard to hear and work through things when emotions are running high. Suggest they access the employee assistance program in your organisation to help them with their approach to regulating their emotions.
You are finding it difficult to regulate your own emotions in the discussion. That is your own frustration, annoyance etc is bubbling up. You feel like you are too close to the situation to be objective.	The same expert from EAP as above can be useful for tips. Use your own Board after each conversation.	You may need to indicate to those involved that you recognise that your own emotional connection is strong. That the best way of helping everyone is to have someone more independent to facilitate the conversation. I recommend finding someone who already has or knows how to quickly find connection with people. This may be a peer, an external expert in facilitated conversations or an HR resource.

LET'S SHRINK AN ELEPHANT

Situation	Informal support	More formal support
One person is digging their heels in, adamant that they have the right view.	How far can you go with finding common ground on which you agree? Sometimes it is an inch-by-inch process where you need to keep coming back to the areas that you agree on. Use your own Board to help you consider how to help them to build trust in you and to frame up curious questions that help them.	You may want to request the person bring a support person along to help them. You may need a formal HR process for whatever the complaint is. An independent person coming in to have the conversations can help. Again, be comfortable that they have the skills to develop rapport.
During the process you realise, or they accuse you of being a significant contributor to the conflict.	Seek your own Board out on this to reflect. Sometimes being part of it, showing others how you are curious and reflective through this, can fast track others to become reflective and own their part.	It depends how serious the situation is as to whether this support is another manager, an expert in facilitated conversation or an HR Partner. Your Board can help you with this.
They choose to engage a lawyer.*	This does not automatically mean you should too. It very much depends on the situation. When lawyers get involved on both sides it can become costly and detached from what you are trying to do here. Connect as human beings. Keep tuning into yourself and your language so you are using connecting language. Reach out to the lawyer proactively. You may be surprised how you can find that connection with the lawyer the person has engaged. Having a three-way conversation can be helpful between you, the person and their lawyer.	You may consider having a lawyer as an informal sounding board but do engage them via HR to get the right skill set. If you engage them, stay tuned to what you know is right in how to treat others. Lawyers are more focused on the legal process than deeply understanding what it takes to help people to understand, accept, and move forward. When the other lawyer is clearly aggressive, then engaging a lawyer on your side is unfortunately what is required. Do not lose sight though of the value of continuing to make connection bids to the actual person. Keep letters to that person warm and welcoming of connection as they will be in a world of pain and loneliness when they have reached this point.

* The information in this table does not constitute legal advice. Please seek your own legal advice, based on your personal circumstances.

rienced person, who can get people comfortable and guide the conversation. They are a useful resource, to have up your sleeve.

This section is not designed to go into the legal definitions of situations, nor provide you with legal advice. You need to accept you operate in a world of grey. Not black and white. Sometimes, because of the situation, further help is needed. But you need to tread carefully. Stay true to your own role, throughout this. Keep consciously finding ways of triggering oxytocin and serotonin in others and yourself. Lead the way, remaining open and curious to the multiple truths that will come up. Seek legal advice where needed, but do not outsource your role in caring for your team.

What is different in my approach, when I find myself amid conflict?

When you find yourself involved directly in conflict, your ability to keep staying curious can be tested. You can still modify some of the approach outlined previously, but you need to focus on understanding their story first, before you get yours across. You need to identify quickly, where you need additional support.

When you find yourself in conflict with a peer, you want to keep staying curious, to get them to consider options that work for both of you. If you can have this conversation the moment differences appear, the stronger your relationship can become. When this isn't working, be transparent with them on the need for help. Help could be:
- getting a peer or manager involved, using the approach in this book.

- using an independent expert in facilitated conversation or an HR resource.

Throughout, you need to use your Board effectively, to keep eliciting those balancing chemicals, so you can stay curious.

When the conflict arises between you and your manager, and you can't seem to be able to get them curious enough to explore different perspectives, consider:
- Using your Board to reflect hard on yourself. What are you blind to? What might you need to shift in your behaviour to make this work? Are you comfortable doing this?
- Is this a case of your manager's style not bringing out the best in you? Are their blind spots too large for you to help them shrink them? Is this a values clash that has you reconsidering your role?

Your health isn't worth being damaged to 'fit in' with a manager's values and style that doesn't work with yours. If someone isn't open to truly connecting and learning different perspectives of the elephant, it may be time to consider what your next career move may be. To a place which brings out your best. Where you can do the same for others.

Will the elephant shrinking methodology always work?

The short answer is no. The longer answer is you always have options. Consciously choosing each step of the way, is what matters. This methodology consistently works if you, as the manager who ultimately the two conflicting parties report to, is willing to have the conversations. When you have a leader who doesn't want to, or doesn't see the need to talk openly, then you have other options to take.

I have had two very different experiences in dealing with unresolved conflict at peer level, with managers who were not capable of facilitating these conversations. It was quite clear, in both circumstances, that my peer was not interested in talking through anything to find a way to resolve the differences. They were focused on their own needs and desires above others. In the first case, they directly stated a lack of interest in talking. In the second case, they found ways of rationalising avoiding the conversation. In both cases, two very different managers above did not want to engage in the resolution. In taking the view of 'everyone is doing the best they can with what they have', I could recognise that neither of my managers had the skills to navigate conflict effectively. One was the ostrich who just wanted me to solve it. In the other case, the manager was a bull in a china shop, who thought conflict, in all its forms, was good. In the first situation, I was able to recognise, that while I didn't love having this dysfunctional person as a peer, I could continue to function effectively with my own teams, without their business area's input. So, I chose to stay, with a workaround that worked for me and my team. I recognised in the second situation, that unless I played the same 'game' my peer and manager were playing, I would not be able to effectively work in this team. So, I chose to move. In both cases, I had choice, and I exercised it.

The techniques in this book can be used just as effectively with your peers or manager. With the caveat around the level of insight your manager has. In many situations, you will be able to use these techniques and shrink elephants together. Where peers lack insight, but the manager above you is able to have these conversations, then again, these techniques work well. When you need to involve your manager and they aren't comfortable, it gets harder. But it is still worth trying. Where your manager doesn't have the insight, you can choose your next career move, having learnt more about yourself and becoming a better leader through this.

Key things to remember

In recapping what you have covered in this chapter, here are the key things to remember:
- **There is never one contributor to persistent conflict being present.** There will always be multiple layers of causation. From the systems, processes and policies and their interpretation; to the culture; to the skill sets of those involved; to people's past trauma; to everyone's allostatic load. There is never one answer to 'the cause'. There are always multiple truths.
- **If you stop too early in your inquiry into causation, you are only putting a band aid on an infected wound.**
- **People, including you, can get stuck in their stories and believe they are right.** It is important to stay curious, to understand all the things that have contributed.
- A **caring scientist approach helps** to challenge yourself to provide care, while curiously seeking for alternative answers, to the stories that come up.
- You have a toolkit of questions to help you in this process.
- You got introduced to the concept of restorative justice. How unearthing everyone's stories, **so they feel seen, heard and**

that they matter, is at the heart of enabling both parties to own their story and move forward .
- You have a toolkit of questions that you can apply, to enable 'restorative justice' in practice.
- You have a guide for when you need to involve others (informally or formally) to help guide you through.
- And finally, you have considered how to approach it slightly differently when you find yourself caught in the conflict itself, where you always have options for your next move.

In all of this, it is important to accept your own biases. Then help others to accept that their truth is absolutely their experience AND that there are other perspectives on the elephant. Conflict provides a great opportunity to learn about yourself and others. In doing so, people become more effective at recognising their stories. How to process the strong emotions bubbling up, to then move forward. The more you help the team practise this, with what I would call 'minor scuffles', the more willing they will be to face the bigger ones. The more able they will be to accept that there could be a different story to the one in their head, that may be just as valid. Amid the different lenses, is a 3D elephant all parties can own to move forward.

As you may have already experienced though, despite all of this, the level of chronic cortisol for people may lead to completely deteriorated relationships with formal accusations of inappropriate behaviour. The next chapter explores the critical role you play as a leader remaining in the driver's seat of maintaining relationships throughout a formal investigation.

SECTION THREE

CAN YOU STAY CURIOUS WHEN IT'S BIG ?

CHAPTER SEVEN

WALKING WITH BIG ELEPHANTS

'I am waiting until we know the outcome of the investigation'

This is one of those responses I have always dreaded, in my conflict coaching work. When I have been asked to step in, on a complicated Workers' Compensation claim for stress, my first step is to check in with the manager of the person involved. I want to understand their relationship with this person. How often they are speaking to them. This response of waiting to contact their team member, has frustration bubbling up in me. What irreparable damage has been done by not connecting?

There can be a level of relief when you call in help and it becomes a formal process. It is natural to think you have the experts in now. They can tell you what to do. How it all works. Particularly, if you haven't dealt with an issue like this before. You would assume that they will know exactly what to do. Unfortunately, they won't know the nuances of the people involved. They will be focused on investigating to determine a legal position and 'manage' the risk. They don't have the role of maintaining close connection with all those involved.

The role of leadership is juggling those three balls: Task, Team, and Self.

> *In a formal investigation into people in your team, the investigator only has a task ball. It is you that still holds all three balls of leadership.*

Despite the best of intentions from those conducting investigations, they take time. This is primarily due to managing diaries between all the people involved. It also takes time, for the person investigating, to write up a report and have it reviewed and finalised. In that time, the person making the complaint, or having the complaint levelled against them, sits in limbo land. For the pattern seeking brain of people at the centre of the conflict, when they hear nothing, cortisol runs rife. Their brain fills the silence with stories.

> *The stories that get stuck in people's heads are what make resolving conflict more and more difficult.*

Elephants become unwieldy when investigations take too long. The stories that fill the silence, can reinforce for that person, that their perspective of the elephant is the only right one. You need to have the confidence to help guide the process.

In this chapter I will help you understand:
- The critical role you play, versus the experts, during a formal investigation.
- What makes for a good investigation. Not so you could be an expert investigator. Rather, to help you know what it should feel like for you and those involved.
- Where the pitfalls in a formal investigation exist. Including an unavoidable situation of people not feeling psychologically safe during it and what you can do about it.
- Finally, we will explore the impact on your team, when these events are taking place. People don't exist in isolation from the rest of the team. The silence for the team also gets filled with stories and the elephant grows even bigger. The last section explores how you can shrink team elephants. Maximising opportunity for skill development.

Where should I focus my energy when others are leading the investigation?

Clarity of roles is always good to have in any investigation, to ensure its effectiveness. Even more so where there are heightened emotions. When you don't have clarity, you risk tripping over each other or leaving gaps, with assumptions of what another party is doing.

Depending on your organisation, you may have someone internal conduct a formal investigation, or it may be an external person. Where there is an external person, it would typically be someone in HR who engages that investigator. What I find helpful in defining roles, is to think about the questions each role needs to answer. Understand your role.

The investigator has the role of answering the questions:
- What are the established facts?
- Was there a breach in policy/code of conduct or the law?
- If there is a breach, what is the recommendation to address this?
- If there is a potential crime that has been committed, what needs to be done to involve the police?

The HR role, (again depending on size of organisation, could be the same person as the investigator or your business partner) answers the questions:
- Is everyone clear on the agreed process to follow?
- Has legal privilege been put in place where required?
- Is the process being followed?
- Is the business reputation being protected?
- Does anyone involved need additional support?

Your role:
- Are you comfortable everyone is aware of the process and their role in it?
- How well do you know each party? And what is the best way of you keeping in touch with them throughout? This can include a regular diarised catch-up face to face, regular calls, and texts. Do not underestimate the importance of the face to face in this. You are wanting to keep eliciting oxytocin and serotonin in them. This is far easier done face to face.
- If the 'other party' is outside your team, then is the other leader aware of their role in supporting 'their person'? What will your rhythm of catch up be with this other manager, to maintain a common understanding of emerging perspectives of the elephant?
- Are HR, and the investigator, playing the roles they need to play? If not, follow up to hold to account on timeframe and process, to help advocate for those involved.

- Can you see signs of one party 'digging in their heels' on being 'right'? If so, how can you elicit more oxytocin and serotonin in how you talk with them? Help them breathe through their 'rightness' and start to get curious about the possibility of multiple truths. To be clear, this includes during debriefs with HR/ the investigator. They too can get stuck in one story. Curiosity is the key here.
- When you are digesting outcomes at the end and choosing to implement recommendations, take the time to reflect on them. What do you think? Does that sit/feel right? What would you vary? Will this be career limiting for someone? Who suffers most in a team move, if that is a recommendation? What's the teaching opportunity in this? What can everyone learn that is valuable? What might you need to do differently?

Leadership is about bringing out the best in others. This is tough during an investigation, where cortisol is running rife for those involved in the conflict. No matter how uncomfortable it can be for you, it is important to stay connected to those involved.

It is worth checking in with your own HR team, to understand the current process in your organisation. Find where you might get resistance on roles, should a formal investigation take place. This enables you to influence now, how people think about getting the best out of an investigation. Rather than in the thick of an investigation itself.

What makes for a good investigation?

Good investigations, at their heart, are about curiously exploring all those layers of the ecosystem, helping to tease out where possible contributors lie. Where it is never a black and white answer to causation. It can take years of doing these investigations to build up the skills in 'sensing the system'*, to appreciate how it contributes. I do not expect you to be an expert in being an investigator who is able to 'sense the system' quickly. It is important though, for you to recognise that investigations can become clinical. They can be conducted in a way that is technically correct, determining if there is a legal/policy question to answer to, but not helpful in effectively shrinking the elephant. Investigators can get caught up in a black and white process, missing the nuances of the world of grey, in which the elephant has grown.

A good investigation shrinks the elephant, in a way that helps move everyone forward, with better relationships and skills. Even when it is a significant issue.

A good investigation enables natural justice. It enables all those involved to feel heard. It is a process that is transparent and reasonable. It minimises bias (or rather is aware of it and has strategies to counter act it). It enables decisions to be made with clear evidence.

When you find yourself in an investigation, use the Practical Steps suggestions on 'what good looks like' to reflect on how you and others are experiencing the investigation.

I want to emphasise the last point in the Practical Steps, of *all* parties being supported. You don't want a situation, where the person who is the 'victim' is supported, but the person being accused isn't. Sometimes, there is an assumption that the person

---

* Scharmer, O. and Kaufer, K. (2013). Leading from the Emerging Future: From Ego-system to Eco-system Economies. Applying Theory U to Transforming Business, Society and Self. Berrett-Koehler Publishers, Inc. CA. USA.

PRACTICAL STEPS:
A checklist of what looks good in an investigation
- Can you and everyone involved, explain what their role is? What the process is going to entail? The approximate timeframe from beginning to end?
- Are you and those involved, kept informed, throughout the process, on relevant information and progress, without having to prompt?
- Where timeframes look like they may drift, is the investigator proactively reaching out to apologise for the delay? Then resetting the timing expectation? (Think about this as the brains involved being provided a pattern of certainty, even in change, which helps them feel as safe as possible in these circumstances.)
- Are you and everyone involved, feeling that the investigation is progressing in a reasonable time frame? As time goes on, people become more convinced of their own story. The more they will unconsciously fill in the blanks with what might be happening. The more efficient the investigation can be, the better.
- Can you see the investigator helping people to remain curious? Are they aware of their own biases? Are they managing them?
- Have you got a rhythm with your team member/s on eliciting oxytocin and serotonin throughout?
- Where relationships have broken down with you, do you have someone who is playing this support role and keeping you informed?
- What role are you playing in helping maintain curiosity?
- Is the investigator able to sift fact and identify the multiple truths? That is, unearth both the conscious and unconscious stories of what is going on for all parties? Are they able to clearly identify what is factual evidence versus perspectives on a situation?
- Is everyone feeling heard through this process?
- Are all parties being supported through the process?

(typically more senior), will be ok. That is, they are experienced enough to know how to look after themselves. Or I hear people say, 'if you have done nothing wrong, you have nothing to fear.' Sometimes, it is reasonably clear up front, that one person has done something wrong. If this is particularly abhorrent, they too can be 'left out to dry' with almost a 'they don't deserve our support if they have broken the law'. But they are human too.

A good investigation ensures everyone involved in the conflict gets support throughout.

You need to find the right person to support each of those involved. The person who cares deeply about the individual, but still connected to the workplace. They help elicit the oxytocin and serotonin needed, to then enable the person to get curious about the multiple truths. This is not just a referral to a stranger at the end of a line in an employee assistance program. For those involved in your team, you can only abdicate this role, if the relationship with you is broken down.

Clearly if there is a legal issue and police get involved, this takes on a whole new process that is out of your control. But how YOU make people feel throughout the process is not out of your control. Keep anchoring to that. How can you continue to help your team to keep balancing out that cortisol, regardless of the process, so they have the best chance of not getting stuck in their own story? Help them accept multiple truths through your support.

What can I do if a formal investigation gets unstuck?

The five common investigations pitfalls are:
- **Investigators don't take/aren't given enough time.** They don't really get underneath all the layers of the ecosystem and the lenses people wear.
- **Investigators take too long.** Meaning that memories are being entrenched. This leads to each party believing they have the only truth, growing the elephant even more.
- **The investigator hasn't become aware of their own unconscious bias.** Common patterns from prior investigations can creep in. They don't consider the nuance of the individuals involved. Therefore, they don't unearth enough of the multiple truths, to get to root cause.
- **The right support isn't present for ALL those involved.** While we already know people likely won't feel psychologically safe during an investigation, cortisol left unchecked, can quickly escalate a situation.
- **You accept the recommendations without doing your own testing** on what is best for those involved and the team.

In all these pitfalls, the outcome is the same. The person or people involved do not feel heard, seen and valued. When people feel that way, the recommendations that are put forward are at best a band aid on a festering wound. At worst, they make the wound bigger straight away. Creating an elephant that may never shrink. While a formal investigation is a clinical process, the experience of it is anything but.

When you see the investigation slipping into one of these pitfalls, consider the following to course correct.

Investigators don't take/aren't given enough time

This is one to step into, right at the start. Remember what good looks like. All parties feel comfortable with the process. Check in with how you and those involved feel about the timing. Where there is discomfort, raise this with HR in a curious way.

> *'Can you help me understand what is driving the current timeframe?'*

> *'The current timeframe is feeling a bit uncomfortable. I have concerns that this means we won't be able to fully unearth what is going on. How could we approach this differently together to help all parties feel seen, heard, and understood?'*

Note this isn't about asking for additional hours/time directly but rather focused on the outcome of how people feel.

Investigators take too long

I would start understanding the timeframe, at the beginning. Are you comfortable with the expected timeframe? How does everyone else feel about it? Again, you can use the question *'Can you help me understand what is driving the current timeframe?'*

Raise the concern with HR/the investigator on the risks of an extended timeframe.

Consider the questions:

> *'How could we work together, so that the investigation doesn't take that long? What practical strategies can*

we put in place, to help people avoid filling the silence with unhelpful stories?'

If the timeframe is slipping along the way, then flag this as soon as you notice it. You could try:

'I couldn't help but notice that the timeframe we agreed upon isn't being met. This leaves me feeling concerned that the process itself, could worsen the conflict. Can you help me understand what is driving the timeframe? What could we do differently to get things back on track?'.

Delays can absolutely happen for legitimate reasons. When you see this, all parties need to understand the cause of the delay. You need to double down on your role in eliciting oxytocin, serotonin and dopamine for all parties involved. That is, you need to 'fill the silence' so that people remain curious, not stuck. There could be something you ask those involved to get curious about while they wait. For example, take some time to reflect on what you might be learning about yourself. What are the stories looping in your head? Write them down. Explore what alternative stories could be more useful, to help you move forward.

The Investigator hasn't become aware of their own unconscious bias.

This can become apparent in the briefings you get along the way. Or when it comes to concluding their findings. The test for these biases is how those involved are reacting, including yourself. A simple answer is welcomed as it makes it easy for you. But rarely is conflict simple. It is useful to have the following questions up your sleeve to ask along the way.

'I appreciate the work you are doing here and the insights you are providing. Thank you. I am also curious to consider…

What could be alternative explanations for these behaviours?

What evidence can we find to support each of these alternatives?'

The right support isn't present for those involved

This can become evident when an individual is stuck in 'being right'. Unfortunately, this can happen when someone has a lawyer or union representative present. This support person absolutely believes they have the best interests of this person at heart. In doing so, they tend to play an advocating role. Advocating invariably becomes pushing the view/story that their client/member has provided them. You need to remember, these people play an important role for this person. Particularly when the person doesn't feel like they can articulate their story. The opportunity here, is to help the support person understand how the brain operates. How the story that the person has in their head, is absolutely their valid experience. However, it isn't the only truth. Find a way to build a relationship with this support person. Help them understand the value of curiosity. This is invaluable.

You accept the recommendations without doing your own testing

The simple warning sign is if you are tempted to tell your relevant team member that you are implementing what the report says you now need to do. This is not being a leader. This is being a robot. This is not owning what your choices are. Ask yourself: Do I think people involved have been able to learn more about themselves and their lenses in this process? Do I think the actions here will fundamentally improve relationships (if people remain in the workplace)? Do I think taking these actions will build people's skills in managing conflict more effectively in the future? Are there realities of this workplace that I need to influence? Look at each layer of the ecosystem (Figure 18). Has the investigator explored each of these and their contribution? Do the recommendations then explore what to do, for each of these layers? Are those involved ready to take on these recommendations?

From all that you know, what will move the dial most here? What have you learnt from this process? How are you going to show up differently moving forward?

With any of these actions, you may need to escalate above the people directly involved, to get a needed change. This can, in and of itself, cause conflict with people. Use all that you have learnt in the book so far, to help you connect with other parties, to help them contribute to effective change.

You will not have walked into an investigation lightly. But, if it looks like initiating an investigation was all it took, to get all involved far more open to exploring multiple truths together, don't be afraid to talk to HR about pausing the investigation. (If all parties agree.) Then, return to using the curious questions and restorative justice process in this book, to guide them. Keeping the option open, to return to more formal help, if needed.

FIGURE EIGHTEEN

Sense checking investigation recommendations

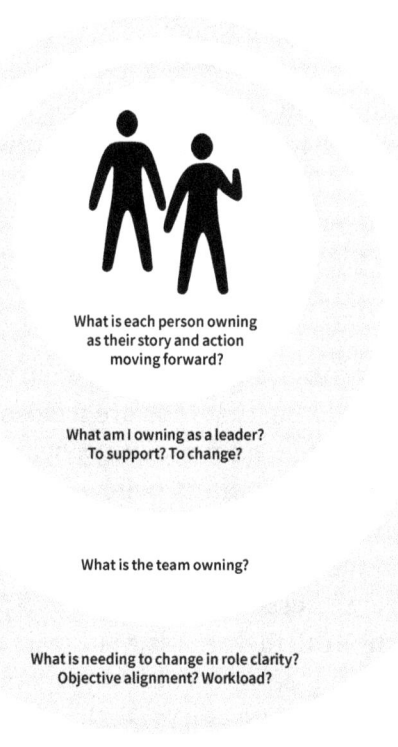

What is each person owning as their story and action moving forward?

What am I owning as a leader? To support? To change?

What is the team owning?

What is needing to change in role clarity? Objective alignment? Workload?

How do I manage the rest of the team during this?

Throughout the investigation, you of course have a day job. Juggling those three balls for the rest of the team. Despite all that you may do to maintain confidentiality, they will likely have varying degrees of knowledge that an investigation is underway. (Depending on their relationship with those involved). It is important to respect the privacy of those involved, in what is an incredibly uncomfortable situation. HR can be quite strong in reinforcing the privacy and 'nothing here to see' mentality, while the investigation is underway. Remaining silent on the investigation or telling the team to get on with their work, while you 'deal with it', isn't enough to stop the elephant growing.

> *The team also have animal brains, seeking for pattern and trying to make sense of the situation as much as anyone else is.*

Invariably in any conflict, people in the team will have witnessed something. It could be, that they are a close friend/supporter of one party. In being a supporter, they hear one perspective of the elephant. They may quickly believe it, because of their own lenses. They may be someone who isn't supportive of one of the parties and will discuss their views with others in the team. They may have witnessed certain things in public and formed their own 'truth'. In all these cases, your team are wearing lenses they may or may not be aware of. They will interpret behaviour through these lenses. They can make the elephant grow with the stories in their head.

So how do you make sure that the conflict doesn't become an even bigger elephant? You need to make the call on whether this is significant enough to have the whole, or part of the team together at the beginning to get people focused. Frame up the conversation with:

**'*I appreciate you will be aware of an issue that has bubbled up recently. I have decided to seek some additional help to work through this. As I am sure you can all appreciate,* *talking through all the details of this, isn't helpful to those involved. We need to respect their own journey in this. I would however like all of us to think about how we are intentionally eliciting oxytocin, serotonin, and dopamine in this team. To help build our ability to recognise and openly talk about the elephants when they appear.'*

What you want to do here, is have them focused on their own actions, rather than allowing radio silence, with them filling in the blanks with their own stories.

The other valuable things you can do with the team include:
- **Spending time with all your direct reports, one-to-one, to understand where they are at,** what support they need to deliver their objectives and how they are feeling about the team dynamic. This is not talking about the investigation. Rather creating an environment for them to talk openly, about what is on their mind. You can help them reshape their stories, as needed. You can help them recognise an elephant can be seen from many angles. Help them accept multiple truths.
- **Establish rituals of connection** that keep the team laughing and feeling valued.
- Think about ripple effects. **What can you action now** yourself or with other leaders/your team, regardless of the state of the investigation? For example, if role clarity is an issue, how do you work on some of the role clarity, right now?
- **Keep demonstrating excellent elephant shrinking skills** when other elephants invariably appear. This helps remind people of what good looks like. To shrink elephants before they get to this painful stage.
- **Focus team on building strong honest relationships with each other.** Shrink elephants together consistently, to build trust for the long run.

Remember, regardless of what is kept private, people will witness/experience things that influence their view of the elephant. If they get stuck in their own 'right' story of what the elephant looks like, this doesn't help you, the team, or those involved in the conflict.

> *The team needs to feel supported and focused on things that help them be better at building relationships. Help them solve problems together. While they see you actively doing the same.*

When it comes to recommendations, determine what is valuable to share with them. What they need to do. What you are owning, to continue to build strong teamwork. Elephants will always exist. You want your team remaining aware, that they only have one perspective on any elephant. Keep them curious to how they can learn to openly share elephant insights together.

Key things to remember

Timing, transparency, and **teaching** are **critical to effective investigations.** An investigation needs to be neither too short, nor too long. People need to understand what to expect through it. A great investigation capitalises on the opportunity for learning for everyone.

Formal investigations can get unstuck because:
- They are rushed.
- They take too long.
- Bias creeps in.

- People feel unsafe.
- Multiple truths are not accepted.
- Recommendations don't address the multiple causes of the conflict.

Good investigations:
- Clearly define roles, process, timeframe, and what success looks like up front.
- Have regular communication throughout the process.
- Help all involved feel supported, to then get them curious about the validity of other truths.
- Address all the layers that contribute to conflict, taking the heat off one person shouldering the 'blame' for conflict occurring.

While you have requested the formal support, you can't abdicate your role. You play a critical role in any formal investigation through:
- Ensuring everyone is comfortable in the approach being taken.
- Staying curious yourself to all the possible explanations/ contributions.
- Helping those involved breathe through the uncomfortable moments and stay curious throughout.
- Getting your team focused on developing elephant shrinking skills.

This chapter has now given you some of the confidence you need to effectively guide others through a formal investigation. Through this you can capitalise on the opportunity to learn more about yourself. I have talked in prior chapters about you recognising the different lenses you bring to these situations. It is possible that the lenses you wear create a blind spot, that finds you being performance managed or accused of poor behaviour. In the next chapter I will explore what to do if you find yourself facing these types of uncomfortable situations.

CHAPTER EIGHT

WHEN YOU CONTRIBUTE TO GROWING A BIG ELEPHANT YOURSELF

I remember working through very uncomfortable performance management, with someone in my team, when they decided to complain to HR about my behaviour. I cannot tell you how much that hurt. Oh, how the cortisol spiked. Here was I, someone who coached others in creating mentally healthy workplaces, being accused of poor behaviour. This was both a tough and valuable life experience for me. I took a step back and recognised the other person had some very thick lenses on. They were unable to see an alternative perspective of the elephant. I could also reflect on where I could have approached a particular conversation differently, that appeared to cause a cortisol spike for them. (Which was already running high due to poor performance). Thankfully we avoided a formal investigation. The HR person stepped in to help support them to feel heard, where I couldn't. But I felt alone.

HR had assumed I would be completely fine. But my animal brain was spiking with cortisol. I felt like I had failed as a leader. I reflect now and appreciate the learning. At the time however, my mental health took a blow. Unexpected, or even expected accusations of poor behaviour or performance management, can have you feeling vulnerable.

Vulnerability, without support, can lead to the elephant growing even more.

Implementing the concepts throughout this book with your team, will decrease the likelihood of unexpected situations. It will enable conversations to happen when the elephant is only small. Leadership though is a lifelong journey of learning about yourself. Every person you interact with is different. Despite your best intentions, your impact may not be what you need it to be.

As you continue to apply the models in this book, learning more about yourself, your blind spots will shrink. But even when you believe you are aware of most of the lenses you have, each person you interact with comes with their own complex lenses.

Each person's lenses interact differently with yours.

They can end up at an opposite side of the elephant. Having no insight into the idea that everyone wears different lenses. Sometimes these lenses mean a distorted story linked to your behaviour. That is, their pattern seeking brain interprets behaviour, in a way that isn't your intent. Likewise, despite your best intentions, you don't always show up as your best. Particularly, if you are under significant stress. You will continue to have blind spots for your whole life. It is important to remain curious to how your blind spots interact with different people's lenses, particularly if a complaint or performance management arises.

These types of situations can be incredibly uncomfortable. It naturally affects your mental health. This in turn can impact your own judgement, and, at worse, affect your career. If you find yourself in this situation, you do not want to go through it alone. This chapter is designed to get you thinking about the practical actions you can take to support yourself, and help you learn through what is never a comfortable space.

In this chapter I will explore:
- Why someone might report that your behaviour is not acceptable.
- Being convinced you are right.
- Who is on your Board to support you.
- Practical strategies to get through it.
- What you can learn from staying curious through this.

After reading this, you may find it valuable to give this guidance to someone whose behaviour and/or performance, you need to formally manage.

Why would someone report that my behaviour is not acceptable?

Your automatic reaction, if someone has accused you of unacceptable behaviour, could be to dismiss it as incorrect. This is completely normal. Your animal brain sees a threat. It wants to protect you. Immediate protection can be to fight. That is, deny any wrongdoing and become defensive. These complaints could be from a peer, a stakeholder or someone reporting to you.

WHEN YOU CONTRIBUTE TO GROWING A BIG ELEPHANT YOURSELF

The person complaining doesn't feel heard. They are choosing to formalise their complaint, to be heard.

A typical reason for a complaint against a manager, is in relation to performance management. It is natural for anyone who is being performance managed to feel under threat. No matter how supportive you try to be. This is a normal reaction. Being 'right' about not having an issue and having a manager who is being unreasonable, is a protective story. Seeking support from others to validate this, also makes sense, to feel safer. The person feeling under threat needs to feel they belong and are safe. They want someone else to see and hear them, when they don't feel like their manager does. They seek validation that their view of the elephant is the right one.

A less comfortable situation, is when someone else, be it peer or manager, perceives you as a threat to their own agenda. You could be perceived as competition for a promotion. As smarter/able to see through their own gaps. That if you achieve your objective, their misaligned objective won't be achieved. In these cases, it is in their best interest for you to not look as good. The theme remains. This is someone with deeply embedded lenses on how they have learnt to survive in the workplace. Them making you not look good, is all about them finding a useful way to protect themselves.

It may not even be as significant as these types of events. Rather, the clash of the different lenses that you both wear. For example, if you are interacting with someone who processes information differently to you (natural neurodivergence). Their view of the elephant can be quite different. Someone may experience emotions differently to you and therefore communication between the two of you becomes difficult. Or someone is deeply traumatised from their own background, with deeply embedded lenses that they are not aware of. That is, this person had an unsafe childhood/earlier life experience. Picking up a particular behaviour early, meant they could protect themselves from threat, by a specific response. As an adult, this then becomes a hypersensitive brain. It sees a version of this same behaviour and perceives a threat, that may or may not be 'real'. They genuinely experience your behaviour as threatening though, with all the physical responses that come with it. It could be that this person has become convinced, due to their allostatic load, that you don't like or value them. Every one of your behaviours is interpreted through this lens. When they don't have the skills or feel safe to have an elephant shrinking conversation, the elephant can get so big, they don't feel like they have any other option than to formalise the situation.

Lastly, there is also the discomfort of your own unconscious biases. Coupled with what your allostatic load is, at any one point in time. You are human. Life gets tough. Situations come up that aren't easy. You may not show up as your best. This is one of the difficult aspects of Workers' Compensation claims. 'Reasonable management action' can be a defence against a stress claim. The debate of course is what is deemed reasonable. This is a grey area. Reasonable is not perfect. This is not an achievable bar. But sometimes your own frustration can boil over because you are tired or distracted or have stories in your head. When your allostatic load is coupled with any of the situations above, the other person's perception of threat can be amplified. There is also the possibility that your behaviour or performance isn't acceptable. However, your own lenses create a blind spot, that results in you not seeing this.

Regardless of what brought you to this point, it can be confronting and uncomfortable. You may feel hurt, upset, angry, frustrated, annoyed or a myriad of emotions. All normal reactions to the threat. If you can take a deep breath and get perspective however, then there is a learning opportunity for you.

As you read further into this chapter consider the following:
- Can you get comfortable with the idea of accepting the difference between what you intend, how you behave and how another person experiences it? That is, can you accept that there are multiple truths about the elephant?
- Where it feels like a relationship issue is escalating, can you get curious on:
  - How has the eco-system contributed to this?
  - What insights does it give about the other person?
  - What patterns are showing up for you in your behaviour and stories? What insight does this give to you about yourself?

But in this situation, I am right!

Before we head into the support you need, let's explore how you work through the initial, normal reaction, of feeling defensive. Remember Principle Two, 'First Reactions Count'. This is a hard one in a formal process. Particularly if it takes you by surprise.

The skill of becoming aware of and decreasing your defensiveness, will go a long way to successfully navigating conflict situations.

What else is going on for you at the time and your own lenses, will influence your level of cortisol. If you already have heightened cortisol, because of other pressures, your defensive reaction could be strong. Likewise, if it takes you completely by surprise. The more you practise being able to regulate your emotions in any stressful situation, the more you will be able to find that gap.

Despite your pulse racing, you need to be able to take a deep breath, (or two or three) and intentionally respond, rather than react automatically.

If you have been practising finding that pause, you may be able to say:

> *'Thank you for letting me know. That's hard to hear and I need to process this. Can you help me understand what is next?'*

In this way, you are neither defending a position, nor accepting theirs. You are just getting through that first conversation, giving you time to think.

Your ability to respond calmly however, may not be feasible in that moment. You may find yourself with a 'that's ridiculous' or 'you have to be kidding me' response. Even after saying that, if you can notice that reaction, you can still pause. You can acknowledge the reaction as unhelpful. Then respond with "I need time to process this. Can you help me understand next steps?". This gives you the extended break you need, to think clearly about next steps for you.

When intense emotions bubble up, it is important to shake them out of your body. This might include:
- Finding somewhere private. Taking some slow, deep breaths. Firmly tapping your sternum a few times, to help reset your vagus nerve and therefore heart rate.
- Going for a walk around the block. Doing some star jumps (even push-ups or sit-ups if at home). Something to get you physically moving. To help get out of your brain and into your body briefly. This helps your brain recognise, that right in this

moment, you are ok, even if there is a challenge ahead.
- Grabbing your journal and writing down immediate reactions, thoughts and emotions. The stories that loop in your head.
- 'Phoning a friend'. Calling that support person from your Board, who can help you take those first few deep breaths. You could even do that, while you walk around the block.

If you haven't experienced this before, think back to when someone was criticising you, in a way you felt was unfair. Reflect on how this showed up in your body. What energy did you use up on talking to others about the situation? Or raging about the person? How relaxed were you going into the next meeting with them? Did you groan at the thought of working with them again? This is the stuff that gets in the way of being able to see conflict, as an opportunity to learn and strengthen relationships. The animal brain, wired for survival, sees threat. Your aim at this early stage, is to anchor the brain back into the present moment. To feel safe. Then, start to get curious about what insights this situation might give you, into yourself, the ecosystem you work in and your relationship with this other person.

Once you have extricated yourself from that first conversation, you need to start thinking about what support you need around you, to help you stay grounded and choose the best path forward.

What does optimal support look like

I talked earlier in the book about the value of a Board in helping to guide you, as you weave your way through shrinking elephants. This Board becomes even more important in the context of any formal process. It is important to decide who you need to support you. Typically, when HR indicate that this is a formal process, they may ask you if you want a support person present for interviews/conversations. Depending on how you are feeling, this may be beneficial. In these more intense situations, you need to consider who has the right experience and skills.

Depending on your position in the organisation, you may turn to a union representative, or a lawyer. While this is an understandable choice, it needs to be treated with caution[*]. Remember your brain will be running rife with cortisol. Trying to find a safe path through. Finding that person who defends your position of being right, can feel like a wave of relief. In certain circumstances, they are needed. They may, however, not have the skills to be able to help you through the whole process. They may not be able to remain open and curious themselves. This player can tend to reinforce your position of being right. Therefore, find ways of discrediting any information that is to the contrary.

What's wrong with this I hear you say?

> *Holding tightly to 'I am right' is not the best course of action for your health, your growth and the most effective resolution of the issue.*

There are always multiple truths about any elephant. Remember you need the right people, to both support you *and* help you see all the different valid perspectives.

To be clear, there can be situations when the complaint is completely distorted. The complainant may need to be guided through their own process of letting go of one 'right' truth about the elephant. However, even when this is an unreasonable accu-

---

[*] Note, this book does not constitute legal advice. Please seek your own legal advice base on your personal circumstances.

sation, keep reminding yourself that they are doing the best they can, with what they have right now. They are stuck in their own story. You can't be the one who calms them down now. This is in someone else's hands. But you can choose not to add fuel to the fire, by also holding onto 'I am right'.

Start with choosing to have the right support around you. People who help you to continually return to a calm, safe, curious mind. No matter how confident you are, cortisol will run rife initially. The goal of support people is to help you get those chemicals in balance. Helping you feel safe. Getting you more curious to what you can learn. What a useful path forward might be. This is a growth opportunity, despite the pain. You need a particular nuanced Board though, to help you navigate this.

In this uncomfortable growth journey, you need the nuanced skills of the space holder, path opener, truth teller and journey partner.*

The space holder is the 'strength' role on your Board. They provide unconditional love and support. What is important here, is that you don't want someone who supports you so blindly that they slip into the 'yes it isn't fair, and you are right' mode. Remember this entrenches you in one truth, when you need to be able to see multiple truths. You need someone who can help you identify, acknowledge, and accept how you feel. They help you breathe through it. While reminding you of the strengths you bring to the table, that you can lean on during this challenging time.

The path opener is the person who sees your potential and keeps the right door open. They believe in you. In what you can achieve. This is your nuanced Seer. When you are dealing with a formal process, you want that person who assures you the door isn't closing. That you have potential. That your potential can become

---

* Anagnostakis, A. (2024). Inside the Mind of a Coach. Part 3. Vertical Development Institute: How Grown-Ups Grow Up. Substack. May 5th 2024.

stronger, by the way you navigate this challenge. They will keep the right door open for you.

You also need **the truth teller**. Look at who normally plays the Serious and the Strength on your Board. In these situations, you ideally have one person, who can play both roles at the same time. It is hard to hear fully, when feeling threatened, but you do need to own your unhelpful stories. When you are in defence mode, you don't want to accept what you may have contributed. You need a deft touch from this person. Typically, I talk about the Serious as being the one who brings you down from cloud nine. They are direct in pointing out the risks with your approach. When you are on cloud nine, you can more easily take a direct challenge from this person. When you are feeling vulnerable, you need a gentler approach. You need someone with a blend of the Strength and the Serious. You need that person who cares for you deeply. Who can see all your flaws and embrace you for who you are. They gently challenge you in the right way, to start walking around the elephant. To accept multiple truths. They can gently redirect you, when you get stuck in feeling right, with only one angle on the elephant.

Journey partners will help you through the process. Note here this isn't one partner, rather multiple. You may decide, given certain circumstances, that you do need more formal support. Such as a lawyer. But you also need to recognise how to contain their role. So that you remain in control of each conversation. It is valuable to have someone who has experience in this space, to help reassure you. That is, someone who has been there and lived to tell a positive tale. Someone to sit in meetings with you, to provide support as needed. To hear what you may not be able to hear, given your own emotions. If they are skilled at making you laugh, then that will help enormously. It is a priceless circuit breaker you will need.

You can't do this on your own. Don't be too quick though, to enlist formal help, from someone who doesn't know you. You may need legal advice. Look to a journey partner and truth teller to help you decide and find the right person.

You may think you will never face this situation. You may not. It is, however, worth reflecting each year, as part of your review of your Board, who would support you through a process like this. Write this down in your journal. It can help guide you in those early days, when your thoughts could be scrambled. It is valuable to know which people you can quickly turn to in time of need. People you trust deeply to support you *and* who can step back and be curious themselves. They will help you learn about the elephant in front of you and help you maximise your growth.

How will I get through it?

A formal process is a roller coaster. Your emotions can shift from meeting to meeting. Your brain, left unchecked, will create all sorts of stories that grow the elephant. Just when you need it to start shrinking. You need practical strategies to get through this, beyond your support team.

Your wellbeing strategy is critical. The classic HBR article 'Manage your energy not your time'[*] highlights the importance of thinking about your wellbeing as renewing multiple sources of energy.

In a stressful time, your energy drains faster.

---

[*] Schwartz, T. & McCarthy, C. (2007). Manage your energy not your time. Harvard Business Review. October 2007.

FIGURE NINETEEN

Your sources of energy. What is your strategy to keep renewing them?

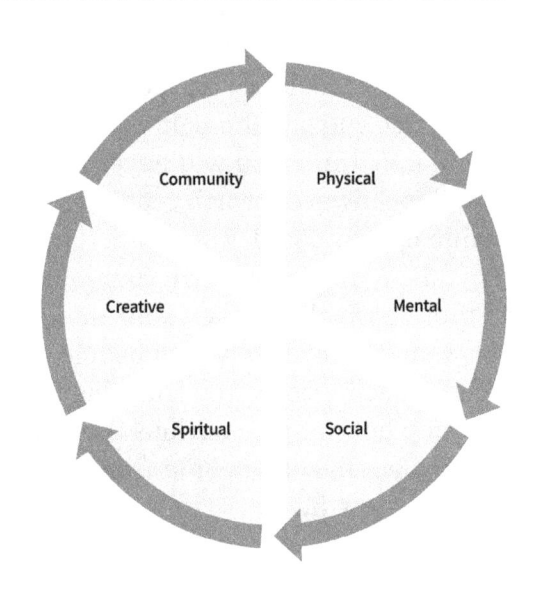

- Community
- Physical
- Creative
- Mental
- Spiritual
- Social

A lack of energy has the animal brain perceiving threat. You will need increased focus on what restores your energy. You may even find you need to add something to the mix in this pressure cooker situation. I find it useful to consider renewing six forms of energy. What wellbeing strategies have you got in place to restore these multiple sources of energy (Figure 19)?

- **Physical energy:** Sleep can be hard to come by if feeling stressed. If you are finding this, then I recommend exercise as a way of releasing tension. This helps induce sleep. Look also at what you do as your bedtime ritual. What helps you get into a more restful space? Consider what you are choosing to eat and drink, so you don't slip into unsustainable coping habits. This is easier said than done. (I am a sucker for eating chocolate and red frogs when feeling under duress.) This is where the Stairmaster from your Board can hold you to account for a good routine.

- **Mental energy:** You don't want to spend all your time thinking about the process. Can you distract yourself, by focusing on an interesting challenge? What interests do you have that stimulate you mentally? Things that have you very much focused on the present moment. What work challenge currently fascinates you? An interesting mental challenge can help calm the cortisol. Your brain recognises, right in this exact moment, that you are safe.
- **Social energy:** Who are your tribe? The people that you enjoy spending time with. Laughing with? Laughter is critical to you in a time like this. This is helping elicit oxytocin, helping offset the cortisol. It reminds you in this exact moment, you are safe.
- **Spiritual energy:** This does not mean attending a religious service. Although some may find solace here. This is about what you do, to anchor yourself in your own sense of balance and connectedness, to something much bigger than you. For me, being surrounded by nature helps this. Tuning into the sights and sounds of life around me. This helps remind the animal brain that right in this moment, you are safe.
- **Creative energy:** Beware the 'I am not creative' response. Exploring and creating something new, helps your dopamine in a healthier way than social media scrolling. This isn't about the final product, rather the process. This could be drawing, painting, pottery, woodwork. It just as easily could be cooking, gardening, writing, doing Lego, learning a new skill. Something that uses your hands. That makes you feel alive. Where you lose track of time, because you are so absorbed in it. In that moment, your brain recognises it is safe.
- **Community energy:** What do you do to help others? Continuing to contribute to community elicits serotonin. Like spiritual energy, it reminds you, you belong to somewhere much bigger than you. Feeling valued during this difficult time is critical to your wellbeing.

I would encourage you, at the beginning of each year, to plan your wellbeing strategy. Start building those habits now. You need to find the ways to keep renewing energy as a leader. It is far easier to amplify those existing habits through a stressful time, than it is to start from scratch, when you unexpectedly run into a very large elephant.

Once you have got through that first reaction to the unexpectedly large elephant, and lined up your support, spend some quiet time up front writing down your thoughts and reflections. What has happened, from your perspective, that has brought you to this point? This is not a document that anyone else needs to know exists. (Unlike formal records on performance management or disciplinary action). Knowing your brain is trying to make sense of what is going on, those initial reflections can help you be prepared for each step and process what you can learn from the experience. Remember though, this isn't 'the truth' but rather one of multiple truths of what has happened.

You then need to decide if you are comfortable being on your own or not for that first formal conversation. Generally, unless there are immediate legal implications, you know you are not at your best, or you have lost complete trust in those leading the process, I would encourage you to consider having that first conversation, without a support person present. This is about staying connected in the current relationships at work. Do however, have them aware and on call, in case you need to pull them in at short notice. Then focus on being fully present.

Post each conversation, write down your own memories of what took place in that conversation. How you feel. What you understand are next steps in the process. How you are going to manage your energy. Choose who you need to talk to after each conversation. You may choose the space holder when you are struggling to get your emotions under control. You may choose the truth teller if you recognise you are stuck in feeling righteous. You may choose your door opener if you are concerned about the impact on your career. You may choose the journey partner when you need to plan out your next move, understand where this could go from here, or believe you need legal advice.

Remember the situation I talked about at the beginning of the chapter? It would have been so easy to lose any empathy for this person and be stuck in 'right'. They did not have the skills for the job. They were unable to see it, despite concrete evidence. They needed to find a job that better suited them. They were stuck in lashing out at me, not owning their contribution. I was also blind to what HR were doing 'behind my back' with them. HR were doing the 'don't worry about it. I'll deal with it' response. Leaving silence in their wake. It was uncomfortable. The elephant got bigger for me. I believed in my skills as a leader. I did not want this to damage my reputation. I could have easily stayed in the 'I am right' corner. Kept trying to find as much evidence to support me as possible. Had I taken that path, I would not have learnt and grown as a leader. The cortisol was spiking. I felt alone and isolated. (Ironically, just like the person I was performance managing was likely feeling). It took effort to understand the unhelpful stories in my head. It was the combination of accessing my support network and amplifying my wellbeing strategy, that enabled me to get curious and learn from it.

These techniques are still relevant even if there are significant legal implications. It is not the purpose of this book to provide legal advice. The people who are your supporters may be different, in this situation. Regardless, you still need to recognise when your cortisol is too high. You need a support network that can help you to explore and accept the multiple truths. You need to have a wellbeing strategy in place.

Do not underestimate the impact an event like this can have on your mental health. You need strong support and an amplified well-being strategy to get you through.

Is there really a learning opportunity here?

I know it is easy to think you are right. Indeed, it could be counter intuitive to consider questioning yourself. Aren't you supposed to be confident as a leader? Doesn't questioning yourself mean doubting yourself? When someone criticises you, it can say far more about them than it does about you. It gives you an insight into who they are and what lenses they wear. But it doesn't mean that there is nothing for you to learn about yourself in this either.

> *'I've yet to be in a rumble, or any tough conversation – even one where I'm 99 percent sure I'm totally in the clear – in which, after digging in, I didn't have a part. Even if my part was not speaking up or staying curious.'**

If you want to be an effective leader, you need to commit to lifelong learning. You must do the inner work on yourself. Learn to understand your lenses, that contribute to growing elephants. This doesn't mean being in constant reflection. But it does mean learning to tune into yourself. Every uncomfortable situation you face is an opportunity for your own growth. It may not be clear in that moment what the learning is. If you can however breathe through the discomfort and get curious, you will be amazed at how you grow as a leader.

Sometimes, what you learn enables you to remove a particular lens and keep it off. Or you learn to recognise that lens and when it is triggered. It is such an ingrained part of you, that it will always be there. But you can recognise it in the moment. Take a deep breath. Then choose a different response. Whether you have the 'ah ha' moment and remove a lens or just become aware of a lens, you are growing as a leader. This will continue to unlock more value in you and those you work with.

---

* Brown, B. (2018). Dare to Lead: Brave Work. Tough Conversations. Whole Hearts. Vermilion. London, UK.

WHEN YOU CONTRIBUTE TO GROWING A BIG ELEPHANT YOURSELF

I recognise I wear a lens of sensitivity to feeling different. To not being understood. This dates to that childhood, growing up the 8th of 9. When I am criticised in a way that I feel is unfair/unjust, I can feel an intense level of emotion that doesn't seem to want to let go. I have recognised, from early in life, I felt like I was wearing a very different set of lenses, to others around me. I didn't want to be different. I wanted to belong. This, coupled with my desire to help people, meant that if I was trying to help someone and got criticised for what was an unintended impact, it was very hard to take. What I have realised over time is that this lens goes very deep. I would love to not have it at all. But I have yet to be able to permanently remove it. What I can do now though is recognise it, using my own self talk to help me release the emotions faster. 'There are no failures, only results'[*] is a favourite mantra of mine in these situations. Because yes, I would feel intensely enough that it felt like a failure. But with that mantra, and sometimes seeking out my strength on my Board, I could regulate my emotions. I could then get into curious mode. I could learn more about how to work more effectively with the other person. That's a great result. As I get older, I am thankfully coming to embrace both my uniqueness and sameness with others. I get curious faster, on how other people's responses can help me learn and influence the eco-system for the better.

When you find yourself stuck in being right, and/or with intense emotions that keep bubbling back up for you, what can you learn about yourself? There is a lens influencing your perception of the elephant. This is what you need to get curious about and learn from. Own your part of growing the elephant. This is the learning opportunity.

---

[*] Robbins, T. (2001) Unlimited Power: The new science of personal achievement. Simon and Schuster, UK.

PRACTICAL STEPS:

Quick guide to getting through a big elephant you have contributed to

Initial reactions count. Consider a response like this to hearing about a complaint:

'Thank you for letting me know. That's hard to hear and I need to process this. Can you help me understand what is next?'

Accept that there can be differences between what you intend, how you behave and how another person experiences it. Accept that there are multiple perspectives of the elephant. Get curious on:

- How has the ecosystem contributed to this?
- What insights does it give about the other person?
- What patterns are showing up for you in your behaviour and stories? What insight does this give to you about you?

You need a nuanced Board for these situations who have had some experience in dealing with these situations:

- The space holder – provides unconditional love and support.
- The path opener – sees your potential and will keep a door open for you to the future.
- The truth teller – gently challenges you to walk around the elephant and see different perspectives.
- The journey partners – helps you through the process. This may or may not include a lawyer.

You need an amplified wellbeing strategy to renew your physical, mental, social, spiritual, creative and community energy.

There is a learning opportunity here. Stay open to it.

Key things to remember

Despite your best intentions, you can find yourself being performance managed or being accused of poor behaviour. This could come about due to:
- Your own **blind spots**.
- Tension building with **conflicting priorities**.
- The **combination of the lenses** the other person and you wear.
- You and the other person's **allostatic load** therefore bandwidth to cope with different views of the elephant.
- **Performance** managing someone.
- You and the other person's **mental health** at any point in time.

Your brain will automatically want to defend your 'rightness' in these situations. This is normal. But it isn't helpful to resolve the situation. It isn't easy to breathe deeply and accept multiple truths. But being able to stay curious is what will help you through an uncomfortable process and come out the better for it.

When faced with this type of uncomfortable situation **you need:**
- A **nuanced Board**, skilled in this area.
- An amplified **wellbeing strategy.**
- The **ability to reset your focus** when needed, remaining curious to the learning inside the discomfort.

In this book, you have learnt where elephants come from, how they grow, how you shrink them through curiosity and restorative justice. As well as the role you play in a formal investigation and the support you would need if you found yourself being performance managed or investigated. Now let's explore how you might scale elephant shrinking in your team to help minimise escalating conflict in the first place.

CHAPTER NINE

SCALING ELEPHANT SHRINKING

Have you ever felt like you were the only one holding relationships together? Teams that seem to work well while you, or someone specific in your team, is in the role? Only to have relationships fall apart again when you leave. I have witnessed this, with major supplier relationships and unions. Relationships where tension naturally bubbles up in negotiations. The trust that is built to enable effective information to flow, is based on the individuals involved at any one point in time. It is frustrating to see them falter, when people don't have the skills to develop sustainable deep trust and true collaboration. As we get to the end of the book, I want to leave you with some thoughts on how you might scale elephant shrinking skills. Skills that enable trust and collaboration across and between organisations. This is what ultimately unlocks value. In the complex world we live in, with increasing levels of cortisol, scaled elephant shrinking skills are critical.

Scaling elephant shrinking isn't as simple as asking HR to facilitate workshops on conflict resolution. It takes more than a workshop to build this capability in your team. To help you amplify your impact in building elephant shrinking skills, in this chapter I will explore:
- Your role versus HR in developing these skills in your team.
- Some practical tools you can use to grow these skills in the team.
- Getting your team committed to lifelong learning.

Why is it my role to scale this skill?

Oh, if I had a dollar for every time I found myself with other senior people, when the conversation was focused around 'we really need people to be better at x' (insert customer service, communication, conflict resolution, leadership etc.). Then, heads turn to HR to solve it. It is a convenient, feel good, measurable action to take. People need to develop this skill so, let's run some workshops. Then they wonder why, post all this investment, that an uplift in skill wasn't seen. This isn't because the training was wrong (although it could be). Rather, training needs to be recognised as only one facet of skill development.

The animal brain, with its desire to belong, overrides anything learnt in the classroom, if it isn't consistent with the ecosystem it works in.

The tribe is where a person feels safe. People can learn something in the classroom outside their tribe. It can make perfect sense. All it can really do though, is teach core principles and, hopefully, some early skill development. Just like a dietician can teach you some sound knowledge around what to eat, and even have you cooking healthy meals in the classroom. Unless you are making these meals back in your real life, things won't change. If the tribe you live with far prefer desserts every day, you will find it hard to stick to only eating healthy food.

Where you spend most of your time, is where your brain picks up the most data about how to navigate in the world to survive.

Think about this in the context of leadership training you have been to. Can you recall feeling how inspired you were at the end of a workshop to be a better leader? Where many of your colleagues were committed to this too? How much of that turned up in practice back at work? How much was retained 12 months down the track? You can be inspired in a moment, but if what you witness from your manager and your tribe is different, you are far more likely to replicate their way of operating, not what the training taught you. (It takes a strong leader to stay true to their own values, in these circumstances.)

This doesn't mean don't do any training at all. You can influence content of training. You can provide context to the facilitator, so they can shape the content closer to the reality that people face. You can do the training at an optimal time. But facilitators don't have the same vested interest in your team as you do. You are the one who can make this stick or not. Your people are watching how you are behaving and applying that to their own situation. This carries more weight than the training itself.

The closer training can mirror the behaviour you are role modelling, the more likely the training will add value.

It all starts with you as the leader. You are an amplifier. You are wasting your time, energy, and money on training, if you aren't taking responsibility for demonstrating these skills every day.

What gets continually reinforced in the workplace is what gets learnt.

You, not HR, own the culture and the skill development of your team. You are the key to scaling elephant shrinking.

It is natural to think you don't have time for something like this. That HR needs to lead this. But you won't ever get the change you want if you do. You cast a shadow because of your behaviours. The behaviours you reward and ignore in a workplace. Your team are learning from you all the time. If you deal with conflict by avoiding it, creating it, escalating it, being aggressive or avoidant outside your team but treat your own team differently, that is what your team will learn to do, to fit in. You can block the value of the organisation because of your choice of behaviours.

What you do, your team will learn to copy, to succeed.

If you don't effectively build strong relationships through shrinking elephants, you are leaving performance on the table - wasting time, energy, and money.

———

FIGURE TWENTY

Scaling elephant shrinking

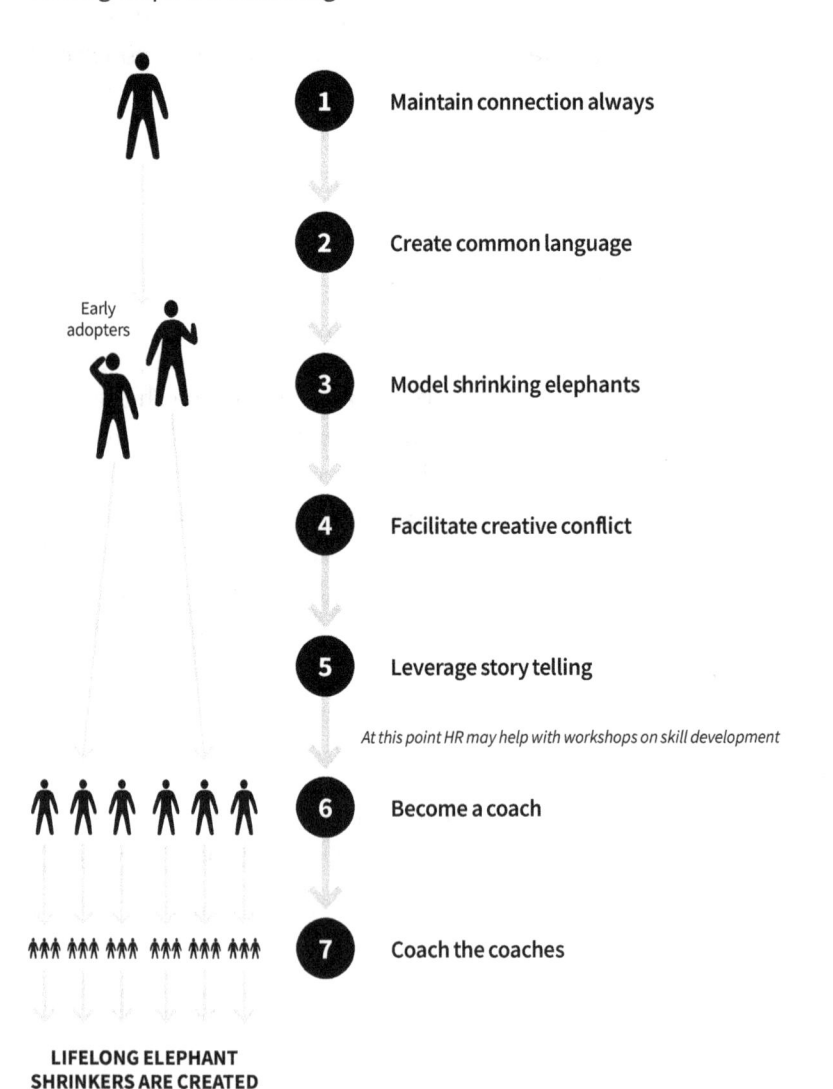

Early adopters

1. Maintain connection always
2. Create common language
3. Model shrinking elephants
4. Facilitate creative conflict
5. Leverage story telling

At this point HR may help with workshops on skill development

6. Become a coach
7. Coach the coaches

LIFELONG ELEPHANT SHRINKERS ARE CREATED

How do I scale it?

Once you are comfortable accepting that you play a role in developing your team's ability, you can then look at what you do to scale it through role modelling, coaching and developing coaches. Let's now work through the steps to scale elephant shrinking (Figure 20). This is a 'you can't pass go' model. You won't get sustainable capability built in your team, until you consistently demonstrate the skill yourself.

Step 1: Maintain connection always

If you can get people to feel safe with you right from the beginning, it is much easier for them to be receptive to your coaching. The start for this is answering the question 'What do we have in common that has nothing to do with work?' Keep reinforcing this connection in your ongoing interactions. Keep using the Five Steps to Connection. This keeps reminding people they are safe with you.

Step 2: Create common language

A common language in the way you talk about elephants makes it easier for people to work together and move faster to resolve conflict. You can introduce language through workshops of course, but they are most powerful when you introduce them into your meetings, and you consistently use them. Consider using the following concepts, in your conversations:
- The **Five Steps to Connection.**
- The **Five questions** to understand someone else's perspective of an elephant.
- The **Five Principles** of Elephant Shrinking.

- The **Five Whys** of 'Help me understand what led to that decision?'
- Who is on your Board?
- Are you in a yellow, orange or red safety zone right now?
- Do you feel seen, heard and that you matter?

You can have some fun with the concept of shrinking elephants. Humour is a great way to break the ice and help people focus on what counts. You could start using phrase such as
- 'Ooh I think we may have stumbled upon an elephant.'
- 'What might a different perspective on the elephant give us?'
- 'Let's shrink that elephant together.'

You don't need lots of buzz words. You need to feel comfortable with the language you choose. Some common phrases, however, create a quick sense of focus for your team.

Step 3: Model shrinking elephants

When you see tension start to build in you or others, acknowledge it. Use all you have learnt in this book to shrink them to a manageable size.

Step 4: Facilitate creative conflict.

Creative conflict arises when everyone understands and values different perspectives. When they respectfully listen to and debate the ideas, that come from these different views, to solve problems.

> *Social conflict comes from people feeling like they don't belong and aren't valued for their contribution. This keeps value under lock and key and risks growing elephants.*

Step 1 focuses on you creating connection within the team. Step 4 focuses on capitalising on this connection, to generate those different views, about the business topic at hand. Respectfully, honestly, transparently. I find the use of Edward de Bono's 6 thinking hats[*], or a variation of this, quite useful. This is where you ask people in the conversation to figuratively wear one hat, then move to the next one, with you **orchestrating every voice to be heard and decision made (you wear the blue hat)**.

- **White hat:** what are the facts that we have now on the situation?
- **Green hat:** what are the ideas around how we might solve this problem?

Then for each key idea:
- **Red hat:** can you each identify and tell us how you are feeling about this idea?
- **Yellow hat:** what are the positives of doing it this way?
- **Black hat:** what are the issues associated with doing it this way?
- **Green hat:** Given what we now collectively understand, what might the best option be?
- **Red hat:** How do we all feel about this?
- **Blue hat:** Let's confirm next steps.

Each time someone goes off track, dismissing an idea, when you are looking at the positives, or defending an idea when you are looking at the negatives, you can gently pull them back to 'wearing the hat' that is being used at that time. This will naturally occur, given the different lenses people wear. Using this as a tool helps people to stay focused on the creative problem-solving process. There are a multitude of different leadership models you could try here. Your HR department could have valuable resources to help you. If you want to read further on this, I recommend reading 'The 5 dysfunctions

---

[*] de Bono, E. (1999) Six Thinking Hats: An Essential Approach to Business Management. Back Bay Books. New York, USA.

of a team'.* Do remember, creative conflict and collaboration won't be optimal, if a safe, connected environment isn't in existence.

Step 5: Leverage story telling

Clearly it isn't appropriate to have your team sit in conversations that you have with others to shrink elephants. But people talk. You influence the narrative inside the team through the stories you tell.

In a team meeting you could try this framework:
- 'I know some of you are aware of the tension that has been building between X and me (or X and us).
- I don't love that it hasn't been able to be quickly resolved.
- Last week I chose to sit down with X to help us both understand the elephant from our different perspectives.
- You see the story I had in my head was…
- This was making me feel…
- What I learnt was the story they had in their head was…
- This was making them feel…
- We had two very different perspectives of the elephant.
- We found however that we have common ground in that…
- We have agreed to…
- This is a good start to working more effectively together.
- What I learnt about myself in this was…'

In a larger team/department setting, the story telling is more about signalling that you have been prepared to face the conflict. That you have learnt something valuable, through staying curious to multiple truths. That is your leadership 'ah ha' moment. It could be along the lines of…

---
* Lencioni, P. (2006). The 5 dysfunctions of a team. Jossey-Bass, Wiley. New Jersey, USA.

- 'When I was younger, I used to think...
- I then found myself recently stumbling into an elephant.
- I found an ingrained way of thinking coming up.
- The story I had in my head was...
- And this made me feel...
- By leaning into having this uncomfortable conversation I learnt that...
- My story wasn't the only story.
- I had only one of multiple truths about the elephant.
- Through the conversation we were able to get to a shared common view.
- By talking openly, we have... (whatever the learning was).
- I would love you to think about your own learning opportunity, next time you stumble upon an elephant.

Demonstrating to a wider audience an 'I do this, and I keep learning' story gives your team a role model to aspire to.

If you want to develop your storytelling skills, I suggest reading Stories for Work[*]. Role modelling of course isn't enough in learning. There also needs to be reflection, for people to make sense of what they are experiencing. This is where Step 6 comes in.

Step 6: Become a coach

To maximise a team's learning, you need to learn to become an effective coach when elephants appear. This isn't about stepping into the conflict for them. This is Principle Five in action 'Understand your Role'. You are not there to solve their conflict. Rather, you are there with a framework for how to understand the elephant in 3D. To enable the conflict to be de-escalated. This

---

[*] Dolan, G. (2017) Stories for Work: The essential guide to business storytelling. Wiley & Sons. Australia.

is about building their confidence. You play a role in asking the right questions, at the right time, to help them in their reflection and learning as an elephant shrinker.

When the conflict is between someone in your team and another team, you may need to then talk to the other manager. To get them to also be a coach for their team member. Collaboratively, with the other manager, you can develop the skills in your respective teams to have more effective conversations. To help your respective teams shrink elephants together.

> *Going in 'to bat' for your team member who feels unfairly treated, doesn't help them and the other person build a better relationship.*

It may 'resolve' the conflict at that point. That is, there is an agreed way forward. But it has weakened the relationship and taught people that the way to resolve conflict, is to get more senior people involved. This is common. It just isn't helpful. Don't get caught in being right or protective of others. Remain curious to the different perspectives. Use your foundation of connection with the other manager to help both of you remain curious.

PRACTICAL STEPS:
Coaching questions to build elephant shrinkers

If someone comes to you, concerned about growing tension, use these questions to coach them through:

Initial conversation
- Tell me about your perspective on the situation.
- Tell me a bit more about your relationship with that person.

- What is the story in your head about that person? How is that influencing how you feel?
- What strategies are you using to breathe through the emotions and get curious?
- Sounds like there could be an elephant here. What might be an alternative perspective of the elephant?
- What do you know about what is going on for that other person right now?
- What insight does your story give you about yourself?
- What do you think is the next valuable step to take?

Framing up their next conversation

- Tell me your comfort level in using the Five components of understanding an elephant from two different perspectives. Would it help to practise it?
- Talk me through it and practise it with me. (They may want time to write it out first).

Encourage them to have the conversation and come back to reflect on what insight was gained. Remind them, that if during the conversation, it is clear it isn't being resolved, they can ask that person to join them in a conversation with you. To get guidance on how to shrink the elephant together.

Further useful questions to ask when they are stuck:

- What are you trying to do? What does that truly give you? What really matters here? Is it serving you? What else is possible?
- What's your current story?
- What could an opposite perspective be? How could that be true? That is, you are helping their brain look for a different pattern than the one they have stuck in their head.
- Who is on your Board? Who might be useful to talk to on that Board right now?

When you engage in coaching someone, do not talk to others about the coaching conversations you have had. It may be the first time you have heard that there is conflict in your team. I appreciate you will want to quickly stop it from escalating. That isn't done by you having a conversation with the other party, to help 'nudge it along'. This betrays trust. You need your team to feel that it is safe to be vulnerable with you. That it is a show of strength to be prepared to talk about these things. If you find out information about someone else that indicates they need help, you can encourage the person you are talking to, to speak to this person. To suggest they too get support. If, given certain circumstances, you decide to talk directly to that person who needs help, you need to plan what you say so you don't give away what you have been told in confidence. Do not give them any reason to think someone has raised an issue with you. This grows the elephant unnecessarily.

As you get the hang of it, coaching does become easier. But it isn't sustainable for you to be the only coach.

Step 7: Coach of coaches

We all learn differently and at different paces. Some people can read/listen to something, apply it once, and take to it like a duck to water. Some, with role modelling and only a little coaching, can develop the skill. With something as uncomfortable as conflict, many will take a longer time of consistent role modelling and coaching to get there.

Lighten your load by developing coaches from the early adopters of elephant shrinking in your team. You know the brain is wired to seek patterns and wants to belong. The more it sees others working to shrink elephants, the more it will feel the pull to adopt the behaviour that others demonstrate. What you want to do, is identify those who adopt the skill quickly. Focus on extending their skills further through your coaching. Recognise them publicly with their peers and in the broader team, for their willingness to step into discomfort and shrink an elephant. This not only signals to the team that you value that behaviour. It raises awareness for the team, of others they can go to for advice and coaching, when elephants appear for them. It also enables you to lighten your own load, by suggesting to people who else they can seek for support, when your diary is full. These early adopters build the pattern of behaviour that others will pick up on. They, not you, create the shift in the team.

Teach them the questions from Step 6. Use one-to-one time with them, to reflect on how they are developing their skills in using these questions effectively. All it takes is for you to start the snowball rolling. As others commit to lifelong learning, the momentum in this skill will build.

Creating lifelong learners

When people are aspiring leaders, early on in their journey, there is a tendency to want to prove that they can do this. That they have the skills. So that they can continue to progress their career. I know I was like this. The risk is that people can believe that leadership is a skill where you get to a certain point and know how to do it. But your responsibilities and environments change. Your lenses can evolve. You get presented with people with such a wide variety of lenses. These produce all sorts of weird and wonderful elephants. To not keep evolving, means you fall behind. Leadership learning is never finished. Evolution of leadership, to unlock more value, comes from reflection, and it is this habit you want to ingrain in your team.

Great leaders remain curious to learning for their lifetime.

Journalling is a powerful way of reflecting. It helps you remain curious and absorb learning. Not just because of the value of writing things down in the first place, but also through keeping a record you can go back to later. I have been journalling for years, and what I have found incredibly valuable in going back is twofold:
1. I realise I have learnt some useful skills along the way. Some things that were challenging me in the past, don't challenge me in the same way anymore. I am more comfortable with navigating these situations now with embedded skills.
2. It shows me where my inbuilt deep lenses keep showing up. Where the same theme comes up again and again. I can then intentionally choose counterbalance strategies, using my Board, my peers and my team, to help me to avoid getting into 'righteous' mode.

Creating a discipline of regular reflection helps the brain to process what has taken place and make sense of it.

In a complex world, you want everyone in your team to be lifelong learners. It makes your own role easier if they can develop these skills. It unlocks their potential. Creating these lifelong learners follows the same principles as building up that skill in elephant shrinking in the first place.
- Talk about both your practice of reflecting and things you are learning about yourself in team meetings and one-to-one conversation.

- In your one-to-one time with your own team, ask them to reflect on something they are grappling with and what they are learning about themselves in the process.
- Encourage people to use this reflective process for themselves with a journal.

PRACTICAL STEPS:

Questions to help the reflection process of lifelong learning

- What happened?
- What was my intent? My mindset going in? My level of effort and energy?
- What went well? And not so well?
- What story is in my head about how I and others contributed to this situation?
- How do I feel about it?
- What conversations do I need to have now?
- What would I do the same and differently next time?
- How would I frame up my next elephant shrinking conversation?

Key things to remember

You can't do this alone if you want to seriously unlock value in your organisation. You want to have a team of people who can effectively shrink elephants. To see manageable 3D versions of elephants. To then use these different perspectives to help solve

the complex work problems you face and maximise opportunities. In this chapter you have learnt:
- **What people learn in the classroom unravels quickly if you aren't role modelling the behaviour you want to see.** Don't waste your time on HR workshops if you aren't prepared to stare in the mirror at your own behaviour.
- **Most of people's learning happens on the job.** You can fast track learning by:
  - Modelling the **Five Steps to Connection**
  - Using a **common language** to talk about the lenses you all wear and the idea of shrinking elephants to a manageable 3D perspective.
  - **Modelling using the Five components of understanding an elephant** to help understand the little elephants as they appear before they grow to an unmanageable size.
  - **Facilitating creative conflict.** Exploring a problem/opportunity respectfully from all the different views of the elephant, without creating unnecessary social conflict. (The feeling of not belonging or being valued.)
  - Leveraging storytelling to reflect on learnings you have had from elephant shrinking.
- Learning is consolidated through reflection. Become an elephant shrinking coach to guide this reflection by:
  - Not racing in to solve conflict/defend your team.
  - **Using great questions to get them thinking differently** about how to approach a situation.
  - Staying curious.
- It is tiring on your own. You need to **find the early adopters, who you can fast track to become coaches themselves.** Spend time helping them become coaches. Role model how you approach coaching, through asking them powerful reflective questions. Ask for their help in stepping into this role. Help them see this as a development opportunity.

- Scale will happen when you get your team committed to lifelong learning about themselves, their stories, and the stories that others carry with them.

Feeling connected, to be able to accept multiple truths, is where it all starts. Conflict is inevitable. But dysfunctional conflict isn't. It wastes time, energy, and money. Shrinking elephants helps build people's sense of legitimacy and their trust in you. You can make a difference in your team, with a ripple effect in your organisation, when you commit to scaling elephant shrinking.

NEXT STEPS

YOUR COMMITMENT TO SHRINKING ELEPHANTS TO UNLOCK VALUE

As we reach the end of this book, I return to my family of 9 and one of those 'uncomfortable' situations. One Christmas a few years ago, we were gathered at our place (just the typical 40 people or so). Some of the grandchildren were discussing we 9 siblings and the 'hectic' energy we can bring to the room. They had started mapping us on the level of hectic energy we had and the level of awareness we had about it, with much laughter. I discovered them doing this and saw that they had put both myself and my younger sister with reasonably high levels of hectic energy but with my sister having a bit more awareness of it. After my initial laughter, my classic animal brain went to 'hang on, what do you mean I am less aware?'. They found this rather funny. This triggered a great conversation. My kids committed to alerting me to when they were experiencing my hectic energy. In a kind way of course. This was such an eye opener for me. There were times when I was so preoccupied in 'getting things done', that I wasn't aware of the hectic energy I was giving off. Their alert helped rein me in. Other times when they alerted me, I got rather curious. I was aware enough to believe I wasn't giving off that much hectic energy, if at all. I could then recognise they were feeling more vulnerable at that time. Their lens of their own allostatic load, combined with their other lenses, needed something different from me to help them. What started as a funny activity, led to great insights for me. I learnt how to show up in a way that doesn't drain my energy AND helps others. Had these conversations never taken place, that hectic energy could grow an elephant between us. Deep connection, trust, and a willingness to be vulnerable in those conversations, shrunk the elephant. It helped me understand a lens that appears for me, that I need to manage. It unlocked value not just in how I related with my now adult children, but also in how I show up as a leader.

Life presents us with so many opportunities to learn and grow. Having read this book, are you now open to this opportunity to learn for life? Are you prepared to embrace courage? To learn your own lenses and the ways of the elephant?

> *'Almost all the challenges we see businesses struggle with arise from people believing they are right about the way they perceive the situation, one another, or themselves.'*[*]

Where are your elephants right now? What have you uncomfortably ignored? What is emerging? What is so large, it drains energy automatically whenever it is in the room? What are your

---

[*] Dethmer, D., Chapman, D. & Warner Klemp, K. (2014). 15 Commitments of Conscious Leadership – a new paradigm for sustainable success. Chapman, Dethmer and Klemp. USA.

deeply held lenses? How committed are you to unlocking people's potential through shrinking elephants together? How committed are you to feel that fear, yet sense the enormous benefit you will get from a willingness to seek a triangulated 3D version of the elephant in the room?

Do you see yourself?

Commit to becoming more aware of and curious about your reactions to different situations. What can these emotions tell you about your deeply held lenses? What lenses can you learn to take off? What lenses will you be consciously aware of being triggered?

> *Don't bottle those emotions. That is internal conflict you are ignoring, eroding your long-term health, performance and relationships by stealth.*

Your body holds onto that tension, storing away the things you won't face into. It will eventually come out in unhelpful times if you aren't careful.

> *'Embodying your leadership potential is an inside out game'**

Learn the contours of your lenses and you will start to see the elephant from a broader perspective. You will become a better leader for it. Commit to lifelong learning about yourself.

---

* Blake, A (2019). Your body is your brain: Leverage your somatic intelligence to find purpose, build resilience, deepen relationships and lead more powerfully. Embright. USA.

Do you see others?

Commit to using the **Five Steps to Connection.**

Build connection in your team as a foundation for everything you do. Work to recognise other people's perspectives on a situation. That there isn't one 'truth' but multiple truths about any elephant. If you learn to find common connection with others, you can come back to this anchor any time either of your perspectives sets off an emotional response. Get curious.

'Listen as if you are wrong'[*]

- How are your lenses interacting with someone else's to create elephants?
- How can you both get curious and build a triangulated 3D perspective of the elephant?

Commit to implementing the **Five Cs of Accountability.**

Do you see the ecosystem?

Commit to sensing the broader ecosystem that you are operating in. The culture, the processes, the politics. The 'system' is not separate to you. You are part of it. You can influence it.
- What might happen if you changed something within your control?
- What might be the ripple effect of your ownership of your role in the ecosystem?

---

[*] Grant, A. (2023). Think Again: The Power of Knowing What You Don't Know. WH Allen. London, UK.

Are you creating a common language?

Commit to creating a common language with your teams. The common language that can help people feel connected, to then get curious faster.
- 'The **Five Steps to Connection.**'
- The **Five components of understanding** someone else's perspective of an elephant
- The **Five Principles** of Elephant Shrinking.
- The **Five Whys** of 'Help me understand what led to that decision?'
- Who is on your Board?
- Are you in a yellow, orange or red safety zone right now?
- Do you feel seen, heard and that you matter?
- Let's shrink this elephant together.

Have you got your Board?

Commit to creating your Board.

Some elephants are easier than others to shrink.
You can't do it alone.

You need the right people around you that you can sense check with. Not the people who entrench you with a view that you are right. You need people around you who help you remain curious. You need people that help you reflect and identify your own lenses and what you may need to shift to help others to shift.

NEXT STEPS – YOUR COMMITMENT TO SHRINKING ELEPHANTS TO UNLOCK VALUE

Can you see the opportunity?

- Commit to the **Five Cs of Accountability**
- Commit to the **Five components of understanding an elephant** from two perspectives
- Commit to the **Five Principles of shrinking elephants**
- Commit to the **Five Whys** of Can you help me understand what led to that decision/event?
- Commit to restorative justice.

It is not talking effectively about our truths that create unmanageable elephants.

While some lenses are not so helpful, others enrich the problem solving you want and need to do. People's perspectives and ideas, from their lived experience, helps provide a more rounded understanding of what the problem really is. These perspectives help solve problems more efficiently and effectively. But first, you need to help people gain a triangulated 3D version of the elephant. This is where the opportunity lies.

The faster you get to that collective 3D version of the elephant, the faster you unlock value.

Elephant shrinking is one of the most important skills you can learn as a leader. I wrote this book with the belief that you can learn the skill of shrinking elephants. That this skill is valuable in improving people's health. It is critical to enabling trust-based collaboration; to solve the complex problems we face in this VUCA world. I appreciate that reading one book won't suddenly make you an expert. I would like to think though, that you are now curious about experimenting with elephant shrinking.

Importantly, I hope this book has helped you to get curious about the opportunity to learn about yourself. To grow as a leader, through understanding more about your own lenses and what truth they create. We are flawed human beings, who have great potential for good in this world.

> *By committing to elephant shrinking,*
> *you unlock the potential in you.*

YOUR READY RECKONER

If you are like me, then in reading through this book you may well have already underlined key points and put a few sticky notes in places to remind yourself of things to go back to. To make this a bit easier for you when you want to start doing these exercises with your teams, here is a 'contents' page for those key exercises. When you need a refresher, I would also recommend doing a quick read through 'Key things to remember' at the end of each chapter.

FIGURE ONE:	The Five Cs of Accountability	12
PRACTICAL STEPS:	How you help people to hold themselves accountable	13
FIGURE THREE:	The lenses that can lead to conflict	16
TABLE ONE:	Practical initial steps to stop the elephant growing	17

FIGURE FIVE:	An entire ecosystem of potential elephants	22
PRACTICAL STEPS:	Becoming curious about yourself and your lenses	28
TABLE TWO:	The chemicals we need to balance in our brain to contribute to shrinking elephants	35
FIGURE SEVEN:	The Physical Health continuum	38
FIGURE EIGHT:	The Psychological Health continuum	39
TABLE THREE:	Clark's 4 Stages of Psychological Safety and the link to our animal brain	43
TABLE FOUR:	The Psychological Safety Continuum	45
FIGURE NINE:	The Five Steps to Better Connection	53
PRACTICAL STEPS:	Implementing the Five Steps to Connection	54
TABLE FIVE:	Navigating common workplace behaviours through connection	56
PRACTICAL STEPS:	Supporting someone with deteriorating mental health	66
PRACTICAL STEPS:	How well do you know yourself?	69
FIGURE TEN:	The 5 components to understanding an elephant from two different perspectives	71
PRACTICAL STEPS:	How can you learn more about the lenses you wear?	75
PRACTICAL STEPS:	Preparing to have a conversation about a persistent elephant	87
FIGURE ELEVEN:	What are your own stories about this conflict	88
PRACTICAL STEPS:	Recognising your own lenses before having a conversation	89
FIGURE THIRTEEN:	The Five Principles of Shrinking an Elephant	96
PRACTICAL STEPS:	Being prepared so your initial reaction to conflict is one of support	102

PRACTICAL STEPS:	Not being a hero: Helping someone have the conversation they need to have	112
PRACTICAL STEPS:	Getting to the root cause of conflict	120
PRACTICAL STEPS:	A conversation to understand an elephant from one person's perspective	124
PRACTICAL STEPS:	Variation on a theme: Useful questions to understand an elephant from a peer's/Manager's perspective	126
PRACTICAL STEPS:	Staying curious	128
FIGURE SEVENTEEN:	The phases of restorative justice	132
PRACTICAL STEPS:	A restorative justice conversation	138
TABLE SEVEN:	What support is valuable when?	142
PRACTICAL STEPS:	A checklist of what looks good in an investigation	156
FIGURE EIGHTEEN:	Sense checking investigation recommendations	163
FIGURE NINETEEN:	Your sources of energy	180
PRACTICAL STEPS:	Quick guide to getting through a big elephant you have contributed to	186
FIGURE TWENTY:	Scaling elephant shrinking	192
PRACTICAL STEPS:	Coaching questions to build elephant shrinkers	198
PRACTICAL STEPS:	Questions to help the reflective process of lifelong learner	203

ACKNOWLEDGEMENTS

I had thought that writing a second book would be easier than the first. After all, not only did I know what I was in for, but I had also taken a sabbatical from full time work in which to write it. Yet, this was hard.

Partly, I found it hard because I was conscious of all the amazing feedback I had received from the first book. In my mind, this book therefore needed to be as good as, if not better and I didn't know if I could do that. Secondly, it was because of the topic. In my first book, the stories were just sitting there ready to be used. Conflict stories however are that bit more complex and I was conscious of ensuring the confidentiality within these. The nature of my career choices in injury management and prevention, has meant I have witnessed and been involved in endless scenarios of conflict. But for the purposes of this book, I felt the need to blend some of these stories, in respect to those involved, recognising the many angles of the elephant and my own blind spots. My first acknowledgement then, is to all those brave people who were willing to work at shrinking the elephant with me. It can be awkward kicking off these types of conversations, but your willingness to get curious and learn with me has been incredibly rewarding. I continue to learn much from these interactions about me and how to optimally navigate this world and have seen significant shifts in you. Thank you for being part of this journey.

In making the decision to then write this second book I want to thank all the people who I talked to about the possibility, for your overwhelming positive response to the idea of a book on this topic and desire to read it when done. It was these reactions that convinced me it was time to get my experiences down on paper.

Writing a book is an absolute team effort. Thank you, Steve, Natasha and Lawrence, for supporting me to take this break from executive work to get my thoughts and techniques onto paper. Without your love, encouragement and laughter, as well as your own different views of the elephants we have encountered, this would never have got off the ground. Thank you, Kath Walters, for inspiring people to write books. What you taught me continues to be invaluable in shaping how I write. To Leonie Green, Rearn Norman and Simon Brown-Greaves, thank you for your willingness to read that messy first draft, being direct on areas to focus on while also telling me to get on with publishing it, for the value that it contained. To Kate Imms, David Venour, Chris Tabois and Jo York, thank you for being my 'guinea pigs' in reading next versions of the book, to help the editing process. Speaking of editing, thank you Felicity Hawkins, for coming out of retirement to do the editing of the book and really encourage me in that final phase. To Eleni Karamihos, Emma Frederick and the crew at Ckaos, it was an absolute pleasure to work with you second time around on design/publishing. As it was with you Maryanna Power and the team at SquareSound to make this book into an audible version.

A big shout out to Ben Crowe. From telling me you had a lot of books to get through before you got to mine, to coming back less than two weeks later to get me on your show after writing Mentally at Work, you have been a steadfast supporter which has been greatly appreciated. To then agree to write a Foreword, before even reading this book, speaks volumes for the trust you place in me. Thank you. Thank you also to my mentors along the way, particularly Diane Smith-Gander, Jennifer Westacott, and Michael Todd, for your unwavering belief in my leadership and potential to have an impact on this world. And to Gabrielle Dolan and Monique Richardson, your impact as thought leaders in storytelling and customer service respectively has been my guiding light for believing in the ability to have impact on a larger scale.

I don't consider myself a writer, so much as a thinker with that microchip of practical action, inserted from my OT degree, and a desire to help people get better connected to themselves, each other and the world at large. A reader, however, I definitely am. It is reading widely on topics and triangulating the information that I read with my own lived experience that has enabled me to write this book. I could thank so many authors here, who have inspired me along the way, but I particularly want to call out Brené Brown and Esther Perel for consistently inspiring me through the impact you are having, to continue with my work.

Lastly, I want to thank everyone who has read my first book, Mentally at Work, implemented strategies within it, and posted on it or messaged me to tell me what the impact of the book has been for you. I wrote that first book, believing the effort would have been worthwhile if at least it impacted two or three leaders in the positive choices they made. Your feedback told me, it has had an impact far greater than that. This was at the heart of inspiring me to write this second book. I do hope you find it just as, if not more relatable, practical and scalable for you to have a real impact in your workplace.

Conflict in the workplace is such a complex subject. There is so much quiet conflict that people are oblivious to or choose to ignore. This is where we all need to get better. We need to recognise when things are uncomfortable and get curious. Having the conversations before those elephants get too big. I do hope this book in some way helps to create an exponential number of elephant shrinkers that the world needs.

Printed in the USA
CPSIA information can be obtained
at www.ICGtesting.com
LVHW091220091224
798490LV00008B/747